Discover Your Roots

52 **Brilliant Ideas**

one good idea can change your life

Discover
Your Roots

Dig Up Your Family History and
Other Buried Treasures

Paul Blake and Maggie Loughran

A Perigee Book

A PERIGEE BOOK

Published by the Penguin Group

Penguin Group (USA) Inc.

375 Hudson Street, New York, New York 10014, USA

Penguin Group (Canada), 90 Eglinton Avenue East, Suite 700, Toronto, Ontario M4P 2Y3, Canada
(a division of Pearson Penguin Canada Inc.)
Penguin Books Ltd., 80 Strand, London WC2R ORL, England
Penguin Group Ireland, 25 St. Stephen's Green, Dublin 2, Ireland (a division of Penguin Books Ltd.)
Penguin Group (Australia), 250 Camberwell Road, Camberwell, Victoria 3124, Australia
(a division of Pearson Australia Group Pty. Ltd.)
Penguin Books India Pvt. Ltd., 11 Community Centre, Panchsheel Park, New Delhi—110 017, India
Penguin Group (NZ), 67 Apollo Drive, Rosedale, North Shore 0745, Auckland, New Zealand
(a division of Pearson New Zealand Ltd.)
Penguin Books (South Africa) (Pty.) Ltd., 24 Sturdee Avenue, Rosebank, Johannesburg 2196, South Africa

Penguin Books Ltd., Registered Offices: 80 Strand, London WC2R ORL, England

While the author has made every effort to provide accurate telephone numbers and Internet addresses at the time of publication, neither the publisher nor the author assumes any responsibility for errors, or for changes that occur after publication. Further, the publisher does not have any control over and does not assume any responsibility for author or third-party websites or their content.

DISCOVER YOUR ROOTS

Copyright © 2006 by The Infinite Ideas Company Limited
Cover art by Corbis
Cover design by Liz Sheehan
Text design by Baseline Arts Ltd., Oxford

First American edition: September 2007
Originally published in Great Britain in 2006 by The Infinite Ideas Company Limited.

Perigee trade paperback ISBN: 978-0-399-53322-8

PRINTED IN THE UNITED STATES OF AMERICA

10   9   8   7   6   5   4   3   2   1

Most Perigee books are available at special quantity discounts for bulk purchases for sales promotions, premiums, fund-raising, or educational use. Special books, or book excerpts, can also be created to fit specific needs. For details, write: Special Markets, Penguin Group (USA) Inc., 375 Hudson Street, New York, New York 10014.

Brilliant ideas

Brilliant features

Each chapter of this book is designed to provide you with an inspirational idea that you can read quickly and put into practice right away.

Throughout you'll find four features that will help you get right to the heart of the idea:

- *Here's an idea for you* Take it on board and give it a try—right here, right now. Get an idea of how well you're doing so far.

- *Try another idea* If this idea looks like a life-changer then there's no time to lose. *Try another idea …* will point you straight to a related tip to enhance and expand on the first.

- *Defining idea* Words of wisdom from masters and mistresses of the art, plus some interesting hangers-on.

- *How did it go?* If at first you do succeed, try to hide your amazement. If, on the other hand, you don't, then this is where you'll find a Q and A that highlights common problems and how to get over them.

Introduction

"The past is a foreign country; they do things differently there."

The oft-quoted opening lines of L. P. Hartley's *The Go-Between* usually produce a smile of acceptance or a nod of agreement, but rarely the question "Different how?"

No one really needs to look too far to discover vestiges of the past. They can be found in houses, in snapshots in family photo albums, even in the stores we go to and the places where we spend our leisure time. Too often, the apparently ordinary or trivial aspects of history are ignored in favor of the grand monuments, the great characters, or the momentous events. Yet it is the ordinary and the trivial that can reveal a wealth of information about life in the past. If they are overlooked for too long there is the danger that they will disappear forever.

Our heritage is a rich one. All of us experience some sense of the past every day. We see it all around us: a local bar, a deserted factory, the local war memorial, the town square, even in the black-and-white films from the thirties and forties shown on television. The past is in towns, in the countryside, at the seaside. Too often we hardly notice it, if at all.

Whether you think you are interested in local history, family history, or community history, the truth is that you are in fact interested in all three—and probably much more besides. All history is about people: after all, family history is about people in places and local history is about places with people. To overdefine either does neither a service.

Your past—the lives of your ancestors—was touched by national and local economics, religion, war, and probably by disease, pestilence, and the weather. You should not be expecting to tell the whole story; just that part that affected you and yours. If this book is different, it is because it has tried not to restrict itself to any one discipline but to introduce a whole range of ideas for you to think about and try to use.

Of all the various avenues of historical study, local and family history have the advantage of being the most accessible to the amateur sleuth. No formal qualifications are needed and the nonexpert is not overly disadvantaged by not having an academic or scholarly background. Enthusiasm, supplemented by a little reading, is all that is required. To learn that little bit more and meet like-minded folks, take advantage of the adult education classes that are certain to be taking place near you, and join a local society. The difference between professional and amateur researchers, between full-time and part-time researchers, pales into insignificance compared with the difference between good and bad research—the only difference that really matters.

Researching your past begins at home. It begins with simple questions, such as: Who were my great-grandparents? When was my house built? The answers to such basic questions are usually easily found and for research in the nineteenth and twentieth centuries no special skills are required. From such simple questions, and their answers, will hopefully come the desire for a wider knowledge of your own personal past. Answers produce more questions: Where did my ancestors live? What did they do? Why did they come here, go there? What was here before this house?

The past starts now. There is often a notion, perhaps resulting from a misconception, that researching the past means going back as far as possible as quickly as possible. Nothing is further from the truth. The "whom begat whom begat whom . . . " syndrome is thankfully virtually obsolete. If that is your bag, don't let us stop you. But you will have a much greater satisfaction from, as it is usually gruesomely put, putting the flesh on the bones as you go. Yes, do what you want to do, but tracing your family back to 1543 doesn't impress too many people these days and it is usually the uninformed who now ask the question "How far back have you gone?" It is how much and how well, not how far, that is important.

Lastly, we need to remember the words of John Berger, London-born writer and essayist (1926–): "We are in our time and they are in theirs." Tempting as it might be to judge and condemn, based on today's morality, ethics, and beliefs, we have to respect the fact that the past was different. The past and our forebears made us what we are—but now is not then, and we are not them. What is strange, unacceptable, and sometimes repugnant to us was the way of the world to them. The rules and expectations were different.

The past may initially appear to be inaccessible, kept remote by an impenetrable force-field of time; we may occasionally only see vague representations of it, as through frosted glass. However, the past is there for us to unearth. That past is our past and hopefully this little book will inspire you to undertake that voyage of discovery.

What's in a name?

Taylor, Townsend, Thompson. We all have names, but where did they come from and what do they mean?

Tracing your past, on the whole, involves looking at lists of names; that is how we recognize our ancestors when we find them.

The sources from which our names are derived are almost endless: nicknames, physical attributes, counties, trades, and almost every object known to mankind.

When communities were small, each person was identifiable by a single personal name or nickname, but as the population increased it gradually became necessary to identify people further—leading to names such as Henry the baker, John the long, Giles from Sutton, Ann of the hill, and Henry son of William.

It was the Norman barons who introduced the concept of surnames into England, and then the practice gradually spread. So trades, nicknames, places of origin, and fathers' names became fixed surnames—names such as Fletcher, Redhead, Green, Wilkins, and Johnson. Initially, these names were changed or dropped at will, but

Here's an idea for you... **Much has been written about the meanings of surnames. Go to your local library and you will find several surname dictionaries, many quite weighty, to put you on the right track. Names are a great thing to search for online, too, and this can be a very rewarding approach. There are also several specialized websites dedicated to the subject, and these will almost certainly cover most of the names in which you are interested.**

eventually they began to stick and to get passed on. New surnames continued to be formed, and immigrants brought in new ones.

The study of surnames is obviously vital to the process of ancestor tracing. However, it is easy to place excessive importance on the family surname in the belief that knowing its meaning or origin may somehow help in tracing your family tree. This all happened too far back to be helpful in researching family origins, although the study of a particular surname may be useful when the investigation points to an area where it appears often. So you can see that only by tracing a particular family line will you discover which version of a surname is yours. It might be interesting to know that your surname was derived from a place, such as Lancaster, for example, or an occupation, such as weaver, but this is not necessarily of relevance to your family history.

Where a study of a particular surname may be of benefit in family history research is when investigation into the distribution of a name points to an area of the country or a county where it is particularly dense. Many have changed their names, Anglicized them, or adopted an alias at some time in the past, possibly for some legal reason, such as complying with a request in a will, or simply because the new name was preferred to the old one. This highlights the fact that although surnames are an essential part of family history research, it is all too easy to place excessive reliance on their origin and meaning.

So, only by tracing a particular family line will you discover which version of a name is yours. It is more important to be aware that both surnames and forenames are subject to variations in spelling, and not only in the distant past. Standardized spelling did not really arrive until the twentieth century. Many immigrants changed their names when they came to America through Ellis Island. Even in the present day variations occur, often by accident through administrative errors. How much of your mail has your name spelled incorrectly, for example?

There are individuals and groups who are collecting every occurrence of a particular surname, and its variant spellings. If your name is among those, then you may be onto a winner. Check out IDEA 41, *The truly obsessed.*

Try another idea…

"O Romeo, Romeo, wherefore art thou Romeo?
Deny thy father and refuse thy name,
Or, if thou wilt not, be but sworn my love,
And I'll no longer be a Capulet."

WILLIAM SHAKESPEARE,
Romeo and Juliet

Defining idea…

How did it go?

Q   **Are you saying that the surname I have now may not be the same as my grandfather's, or his father's, or his father's?**

A   *Absolutely right. Thankfully, most of our forebears were content with the name they had inherited, even if it erred toward the comical. However, so long as there is no intent to defraud or avoid any legal obligation, and if not because of any criminal intent, citizens can use whatever surname they choose (so long as the change is made legally). I had a mother and daughter in a family history class I ran a few years ago. The mother was Mrs. White and the daughter was Miss Whyte—she just wanted to be different!*

Q   **Are there any other ways my ancestors might have changed their names?**

A   *It is important to be aware that both surnames and forenames are subject to variations in spelling, and not only in the distant past. In addition, before the time when divorce became easier and more acceptable, people often took their partners' names to give the appearance of marriage or of legitimacy for their children.*

2

Who told you that?

Family stories abound but discovering which parts are true and which are false is a problem. The answer is to use first-hand accounts as the foundation of your investigations.

There is usually some truth in any family tradition but, if not in all of it, which part? The skill you need to develop is identifying the hard facts from the flights of fancy. What would you make of the example below?

"An Irish cousin told me that my Great-Aunt Christina, an expert lacemaker, made the wedding veil for Queen Victoria's daughter, and came to London from Limerick in Ireland to deliver it."

History surrounds us all. It's all of our "yesterdays," our everyday memories, and experiences. Every day, people tell each other "stories" of what's been happening to them or what they have "been up to." This kind of history—the type that each and every one of us collects throughout life—is called oral history. Some people have been involved in momentous historical events, like world wars or Olympic games, but many others haven't. However, regardless of age or importance, we all have interesting and exciting experiences to share and stories to tell.

More important, historical documents and books cannot always tell us everything about our past. Often they concentrate on famous people and major events and tend to miss out on the story of "everyday folk," often neglecting the multicultural aspect of modern society. Oral history fills in the gaps, but because memories die when people do, history can be easily lost—How many of us have photographs that include unknown faces at an event long forgotten in the mists of time? So it is important that our memories be preserved for all time as a permanent record of how we used to live, work, and feel.

All memories are a mixture of facts and opinions, and both are important. The way in which people make sense of their lives is valuable historical evidence in itself. Few of us are good at remembering dates—we tend to "telescope" two similar events into a single memory or confuse dates and places or even generations. So, when we talk to people while investigating our history, it is important to get them to tell us about direct personal experiences—eyewitness testimony—rather than things that might have been heard secondhand.

The story of the wedding veil is a glowing example of what happens when a memory is passed down over several generations. With a little basic investigation, I discovered that my Great-Aunt Christina was only four years

Here's an idea for you...

If recording memories for a specific project, it's useful to do some background research first. Take a look in your local library or record office at any books, maps, old newspapers, or listings that might be relevant to the discussion you're about to have.

old when Queen Victoria's fifth and youngest daughter was married in 1885, so she was too young to have worked on her wedding veil. However, in 1905 a granddaughter of Queen Victoria married into the Swedish Royal family wearing a veil made from Limerick lace, so there may be a little bit of truth in the story …

Most of us have lives full of hustle and bustle, but hopefully can still find the time to get together with other family members, even if it's only for special occasions and holidays. All family reunions should be seen as ideal opportunities to catch up, to chat, and to reminisce about things that happened long ago, or perhaps not so long ago. This type of gathering can also be a great time to collect and share family stories. Certainly one of the most cherished gifts one can give or receive is a family heirloom, along with the story of the people whose lives surrounded it. Such exchanges leave everyone inspired to find out more.

Do remember, though, that all information is open to question if it's secondhand. Everything needs to be properly checked for accuracy and confirmed wherever possible.

Most of our parents and grandparents have been embroiled in the major wars and conflicts of the twentieth century, either in the armed forces or, just as important, "keeping the home fires burning." So now is the time to ask just what your family's involvement was. Get some pointers from IDEA 25, *Uncle Sam wants you!*

Try another idea…

"There was never yet an uninteresting life. Such a thing is an impossibility. Inside of the dullest exterior, there is a drama, a comedy, and a tragedy."
MARK TWAIN (1835–1910)

Defining idea…

How did it go?

Q   I don't seem to get the opportunity at any family gatherings to sit down and really talk to people. What can I do about this?

A   *Why not organize your own family reunion and get other interested family members to help you discover what memories are held or what family heirlooms, photographs, or other family documents have survived? Make the most of technology: for spontaneous "moments," purchase some disposable cameras and hand them out to volunteer guests, but don't forget to collect them at the end of the day. Film the day's event, which gives you the option of both pictures and sounds. Capture still shots to use from your video if you can. Create your very own history archive.*

Q   What if I don't want to sit down and record my family's memories of other family members? Any other suggestions?

A   *There are many alternative windows on the past. These could be your own home, the place where you work, your school, how people used to cook—anything. Basically, you pick a topic to ask people about: for example, memories of childhood, leisure, politics, religion, or women's experience in wartime, or memories of coming to America as an immigrant. There are many such projects that are already ongoing, and a wealth of information deposited in sound archives, including the recordings of many famous people that you may want to listen to before you start your own project.*

3
Show and tell

From old boxes under the bed to dirt-encrusted suitcases in the attic, we all have collections of memorabilia, ephemera, and documents relating to the history of our homes and family.

Building up a full picture of your family's past as you go along is as important as discovering who your ancestors were. It is amazing how much can be found in papers hidden around the house or in the memories of your relatives.

So, start rummaging for family papers and memorabilia, and recording the memories of those who now possess them. What do you and your family have stored away? Start with yourself before moving on to your nearest and dearest—and remember that it may not be the near or the dear who have the most useful stuff. Go through the trunks in the attic and the boxes under the stairs. Disregard nothing. It may be meaningless now but after a bit of investigation it may hold that vital piece of evidence you need. You are after anything you can find: letters; medals; photographs; a family Bible; birthday cards; funeral cards; old postcards; birth, marriage, and death certificates; baptism certificates; school reports; newspaper clippings; details of a family grave—anything. You are looking for facts and you are looking for clues.

Your big personal breakthrough will come when you realize that most of the apparently insignificant papers and artifacts collecting dust have, as it were, a life beyond themselves. Every item you come across is what it is—but almost certainly it will also be a clue to further sources of research. Take World War I campaign medals, for example. These are going to be engraved with the recipient's name, regiment, and number—all useful references for getting into military records. And birth, marriage, and death certificates will all indicate other family members, occupations, and addresses—so leading to census returns, maps showing where they lived at the time, and possibly records of occupations—as well as giving evidence of migration and mobility.

A trick with elderly relatives is to make them curious rather than suspicious. So try to show some interest in them as individuals—even though it is their possessions you are hoping

Here's an idea for you…

Make sure you look after your family heirlooms by keeping them out of direct sunlight and storing them in a cool, dry place away from any potential danger such as mildew or insects. Try to avoid handling them too much as well. Make copies of documents if you can. There are lots of excellent storage solutions available. Using the proper materials to store your valuable memorabilia won't be cheap but it will undoubtedly be money well spent and you—and your descendants—won't regret it.

to see. They need to know they are going to be as interesting to you while they are alive as they will be when they are dead!

Sometimes a "find" will produce as many questions as it answers so try to get to the bottom of matters as you go along. Birthday cards are great because they might tell you the date of someone's birthday. But if it just says something like "14 May, Maisie" you are not much further forward until you know who Maisie is, or was.

Probably, the most exciting finds are going to be family photographs. For more thoughts on these and what they may really be saying to you, see IDEA 46, *Families in focus*.

Try another idea...

Working with the belongings of members of your family is a very meaningful experience. Talking to those who actually knew those now departed, or have stories to tell about them, is something that can never be replaced by searching the bland lists and indexes to be found in record offices and libraries. But be warned: try to be a little detached as you undertake these investigations or there is the danger that you may be imbued with ideas and thoughts that are a little fanciful.

Every family will be different, but here are a few examples of the things to look out for that may contain some piece of vital information:

account books • address books • awards • baptism certificates • birth, marriage, and death certificates • birthday and holiday cards • cemetary deeds • club and society memberships • deeds • diaries and journals • diplomas • divorce papers • employment records • family Bibles

"Junk is anything that has outlived its usefulness."
OLIVER HERFORD (1863–1935), writer and illustrator

Defining idea...

• insurance papers • letters • medical cards • military records • newspaper clippings • obituaries • passports • photographs and portraits • printed announcements • school awards • school reports • scrapbooks • visitors' books • wedding albums • wills and other probate documents

How did it go?

Q   **My grandmother insists that she has nothing of any use or interest to me. Do you think she might be right?**

A   *Almost certainly, no. Working on the premise that nothing truly outlives its usefulness, you need to persuade her (politely and gently, of course) that she should let you be the judge of what might be interesting. I wouldn't necessarily advocate poking around under her bed yourself—that voyage of discovery may not be entirely what you wanted.*

Q   **I can see myself ending up as the family record keeper but my husband is a neat freak and he won't be too happy if I start a collection of boxes full of really interesting old papers. How might I win him over?**

A   *Try to get him interested in some particular aspect of your investigations rather than taking on the whole gamut. Often those who are not interested in "family" are nevertheless interested in the house, place, or community they live in now.*

4

Is there anybody out there?

You're not alone—there are countless others trying to discover more about themselves or their communities. Contacting them can only help you with your own research.

The study of family history is not a recent phenomenon—genealogies are among the very earliest historical narratives. All you need to do is identify who else is investigating in your area of interest.

Finding others who are actively working on the same genealogical lines as you are allows you to tap into a valuable, usually unpublished, research source. Perhaps they have already covered the ground you hope to tread, thus helping you with your research. In addition, there are numerous everyday lists that can aid you in your efforts to discover these folks.

Try looking in telephone directories or census records for your areas of interest if you're attempting to locate potential unknown relatives. These can be found via the local reference library or, of course, can be accessed on the Internet.

Here's an idea for you...

Tread carefully with your research and do not take as gospel some lengthy pedigree that apparently enables you to claim an impressively long descent from royalty (or another distinguished person or notorious criminal). It is tempting to accept information as totally true, particularly when you see it on screen or in print, but don't. Instead, take this pedigree as potentially valuable information whose accuracy and reliability you have to check and confirm before you incorporate it into your own family tree. Furthermore, don't continue unless you can verify everything you've already collected.

Genealogical societies throughout the world collect and publish the surnames being researched by their members (members' interests)—basically, who is researching what surname and where. These are usually published in book form, on CD, on microfilm, or on the society website. Many society newsletters also contain lists of research interests, offering this service to their readers usually free of charge.

There are also several specialist genealogical directories that are published annually specifically for the purpose of enabling people to make contact with others researching the same names in the same places. These can be purchased as books, CDs, or microfilm. Copies of these publications may also be found in your local reference library.

Always check to see if anyone is undertaking a one-name study of any of the names you are interested in. Often the "one-namer" will be researching all occurrences of a surname, as opposed to a particular pedigree. Although some one-namers may restrict their research geographically, perhaps to one country, many one-namers collect all occurrences found anywhere in the world. Check for these online.

Many commercial and free family history data providers also have the facility for you to record and submit your own family tree to their websites, allowing you to help create one large worldwide family tree. Conveniently for researchers, these are held in a searchable database to allow easy access and show links to potential relatives. These sites also enable you to create your own profile so that other researchers or family members can find you. Many of these sites also host message boards or run news lists. Ancestry.com is a popular commercial site; FamilySearch.com is a great free one.

So, how do you find out more about the origins and demography of the surnames that you are researching? Get some pointers in IDEA 1, *What's in a name?*

Try another idea...

The various publicly available online regional (usually county-based) genealogy news lists, chat rooms, or message boards are other great places to "bump" into other people researching one of your family lines. They are designed to be a practical resource for today's family historian and they are an exceptionally good value as, generally, they can all be accessed free of charge.

Online auction houses, such as eBay, are another place that you can find genealogical gems. Try typing your name or your ancestor's surname into their search engine and see what comes up. You might be pleasantly surprised.

Other innovations on the Internet are the online community websites specializing in finding old schoolmates, friends, or relatives—be they close or very distant—with the of aim of reconnecting relations and generations. Again, free to register and search, but they often have a flat-rate charge for you to access contact details.

"It is a very sad thing that nowadays there is so little useless information."
OSCAR WILDE (1854–1900)

Defining idea...

15

How did
it go?

Q **I tried subscribing to several genealogical mailing lists but found myself swamped with emails. How can I make life more manageable?**

A   *It is worth subscribing slowly to mailing lists—no more than one or two at a time—and being very selective about the lists to which you subscribe. Make sure that you are subscribing to a list that is going to help you progress your research or knowledge. Even within the genealogy community, lists can cover a huge variety of specialities, be it area or regional, ethnic or religious. It might also be better to receive any mail as a daily digest instead of individual emails.*

Q **I am looking into an ancestor called John Smith ... along with thousands of other people! How can I try to locate people researching "my" John Smith?**

A   *When looking at who is researching a particular name, it is very important to look at where that name is actually being researched—particularly if the name is fairly common, as in this case. If you limit yourself to concentrating on those researching Smiths in the same village or town where your Smiths are, it will quickly help you to determine if it may be someone researching the same line or family as your are. Definitely avoid contacting those people who are just fishing and looking for John Smith "anywhere."*

5

Truth and lies

By asking questions, particularly of your older relatives, you could get vital clues about your family's past. However, don't rely completely on family stories before you've cross-checked them with other sources.

For centuries, individuals, families, and societies have been researching families, homes, villages, and towns. And this may be your family, home, village, or town.

It is so important to speak to older relatives while they are still around, but don't stop there—the younger generations may know more or different snippets. Grandparents often have more time to spend with their grandchildren than they did with their own children, so tales of their childhoods and families may skip a generation. My grandmother had eleven siblings altogether, with four sisters still alive when I first started researching my past. Each sister knew something different and would occasionally disagree about a simple "fact." The importance of contacting every known relative is therefore obvious.

It's unlikely that you will know all your living relatives. You may possibly have a name or two for your more distant relatives but not much more. However, it is possible that these are the very family members who will hold the vital clues you will need to progress your investigation into your family's past. Discovering these "lost" relatives needs to be an important part of your initial investigation.

There is an effective trick you can try when talking to relatives, particularly the older ones—slip into the conversation a deliberate "falsehood." This can be especially useful if the old dear is being overly reticent and stubbornly noncooperative. Mention a totally fictitious event concerning a great-uncle, for example, about whom you really want to know more. You will soon be corrected and more real information will often be forthcoming. I have sometimes even made up a relative just to get the reaction "Don't you mean ...?"

How you approach your relatives depends on several things: How well do you know them? Where do they live? Are they on the Internet? Do you personally prefer phoning or writing? The choice is yours, but which method you go for is relatively unimportant, although there is a lot to be said in favor of writing, especially to those you do not know too well, or at all.

You can include a simple questionnaire laying out the problems you would like resolved. These questions can be quite specific, being about names, dates or places, or perhaps a birth or a marriage. You could also ask about what school someone went to, or if he served in the Armed Forces, or what he did for a living. Other questions can be more general, enquiring about any photographs, a family Bible, letters, stories about the family, and so forth. And remember, you can, and should, always go back with further queries;

so don't try to get too much into your initial enquiry or you might put the relative off.

It is important to make sure that the people you are contacting know who you are. If you know very little about them, then the chances are they will know little or nothing about you. Explain who you are and try to reassure them from the outset that your research is just for your and the current family's benefit. Emphasize that you merely want to build a bigger, better, and more accurate picture of the family for posterity and that this is not part of some scam to cheat them out of their inheritance. Many people are, quite understandably, protective of their own history and need to be assured that what you are doing is not going to undermine that.

Accounts from relatives may contradict each other, or be at variance with your own memory. This is not a problem provided you keep a note of where each piece of information came from and you check everything in the records whenever you can.

Don't blindly dismiss those unlikely family stories. There might be claims of descent from a famous person, such as Abraham Lincoln, but, on investigation, you might find that an ancestor ran a bar with that name. Somewhere there is usually an element of truth, however confused. My great-great-great-grandfather may not have been Mayor of Hungerford, but he certainly lived there.

Be prepared for a whole range of emotions, from frustration to elation, but the bottom line is that it will be incredibly rewarding.

While you are asking your family about their memories, don't forget to ask what old papers, photographs, and the like they may have. Take a look at IDEA 3, *Show and tell*.

Try another idea...

"God gave us our memories so that we may have roses in December."
JAMES MATTHEW BARRIE (1860–1937), dramatist and novelist

Defining idea...

19

How did
it go?

Q How can I possibly approach a great-aunt I've never met and expect some constructive help?

A *One way to unearth the information you are after from distant relatives is to send a copy of the facts that you do already have, perhaps in the form of a simple family tree. Most people can understand these whereas if you constantly just refer to great-grandmother this or second cousin that, it is easy for them to become confused.*

Q Everyone I speak to tells me that my great-grandfather was born on 24 September 1879, but I can find nothing to confirm this. Why might that be?

A *Relatives may insist that your forebear was born on that date, but perhaps he in fact was not. The answer is often to look a year or two on either side. You might discover he was actually born on 24 September 1881. Then again, the date of birth may occasionally be found to be exactly a week out, possibly because the registrar misinterpreted "She was born last Wednesday," or there was an error in the transcription.*

6
Join the club

Local history societies and family history societies abound in all parts of the world. Their journals and books are a rich source of help and advice if you know how to use them effectively.

You'll need to understand the difference between local and family history societies to be able to get the best from both in your quest for information.

Family history or genealogical societies promote and assist the study of genealogy and family history. Their prime interest is the study of people and, second, the places where those people live. Local history societies concentrate on an actual physical place or area and are, therefore, interested in the people because of where they live.

Family historians need to be able to set their ancestors in the context of the society or place where they lived—and thus depend on the work and expertise of the local historian. The two disciplines rely on many of the same sources, but apply them using different methods. Family historians need an understanding of the ways in which local historians use records, particularly unusual or unique sources that local historians may have identified. Reading local histories of the communities where your ancestors lived can help you to build on the information that you already have.

Conversely, local historians need the work genealogists do in transcribing sources such as census entries and tombstone inscriptions. They also need their support in lobbying for improved access to records. The writing of family history easily merges into the writing of local history.

Local history enriches our lives, both as individuals and as whole communities. It is an area where amateur and professional can meet and work profitably together. Local historians range from interested individuals and members of local societies to professional archivists and university professors. There are many thousands of people now actively involved in making a valuable contribution toward enriching and extending our understanding of the past.

Most cities and counties have their own family history society or societies. Most larger cities have a local history society while most towns either have a society or individuals who are

Here's an idea for you...

Join a society in the area where you live, even if your genealogical interests are in a different region. By attending their meetings, not only will you meet a lot of likeminded people but you will also find out what research resources are available to you locally.

extremely knowledgeable about the area and its history.

SO, HOW CAN SOCIETIES HELP YOU WITH YOUR RESEARCH?

To see who else might be researching or interested in your family, village, or town, look at IDEA 4, *Is there anybody out there?*

Try another idea...

Most societies produce journals or newsletters containing historical articles about life in the area, general articles describing local records, information about local indexes, and what's new or going on in the area. These publications also list members' interests (who is researching a specific surname in a specific area, for instance), helping members to contact others who share their research interests.

Societies hold regular meetings, often centered around a lecture, typically with an expert speaker. More important for our purposes, these meetings give attendees the opportunity to obtain assistance and advice and meet others with similar interests, all on a mutual self-help basis. Some societies sell books at these meetings, giving the opportunity to peruse the latest book titles. Societies are run by volunteers so they do not usually have the resources to undertake research on your behalf, but they are able to offer guidance on your own research. Some societies also organize conferences and courses that aim at extending your level of expertise. Many organize trips to the National Archives in Washington, DC, the Family History library in Salt Lake City, Utah, and other record repositories. Some societies also have research rooms containing various general family

"There is not a sprig of grass that shoots uninteresting to me."
THOMAS JEFFERSON (1743–1826)

Defining idea...

history sources, transcribed records, indexes, and sometimes historical material relating to their area of interest. Admission to these research rooms is generally free for members.

Genealogical and local history societies have, for a number of years, been transcribing and indexing local records, such as census schedules; tombstone inscriptions; birth, death, and marriage certificates; military records; immigration histories; land tax assessments; and court documents. Much of this work has been published in various formats including book, microfilm, and CD, and it is sometimes available to purchase or view on the Internet.

Q   Are there any special interest family history societies?

A   Yes, there are societies covering special areas of research such as German Americans, Italian Americans, Catholics, Native Americans, Jewish families, Quakers, railroad workers, and many other groups. There is also another special type of "society"—a one-name study. A one-name study is a project researching all occurrences of a specific surname. These may concentrate on aspects such as geographical distribution of the name and the changes in that distribution over the centuries, or may attempt to reconstruct the genealogy of as many lines as possible bearing the name. One-namers often make an attempt to quantify the rarity of their name. A coopera-tive effort between people studying the same surname bears much fruit and the people involved have a good chance of discovering new relatives, depending, of course, on how common the name is.

Q   How do you locate the contact details of a society?

A   Your local archive, record office, or library should have a list of societies and history experts based in your area. They should also be able to inform you of specialized publications that give societies' full contact details. Check, too, if the society in your area of interest has a website.

How did it go?

25

7

Hatches, matches, and dispatches

Since the mid-twentieth century, the government has been officially recording births, marriages, and deaths. Join us to glean the most from these records.

You'll be pleasantly surprised at what you can dig up in the vast number of documents housed in the Office of Vital Records for your area of interest.

Vital records have proved to be a treasure trove of information for family and local historians, helping to verify events and also fill in the gaps in our family trees. Even as we go through our own lives, we increasingly need certified copies of our own birth or marriage certificates to prove who we are or who we are married to. When we die we cannot be buried or cremated without having a death certificate.

Here's an idea for you... **If your ancestor was born before civil registration commenced or you are unable to locate their birth in the indexes, try to locate the birth certificate of a sibling, which will give you the same information that you require to advance your research.**

Try another idea... **The name of an ancestor and which state they resided in is enough information to begin a census search.**

Defining idea... *"It is a mistake to try to look too far ahead. The chain of destiny can only be grasped one link at a time."*
WINSTON CHURCHILL (1874–1965)

The basic information provided varies by location and time period. Birth certificates give the date and place where the event occurred, the child's forename(s), the name of the father, and the name and maiden surname of the mother, and may contain the name and address of the witness for the registration. A marriage certificate gives the names and usually the ages of the marrying couple, their addresses, the name and occupation of the groom, the date and place of marriage, and the names of the witnesses. Death certificates record name, date, place, age, cause of death, residence if different from the place of death, and the name and address of the informant for registration.

More important, apart from giving you the basic information that helps you to go back another generation, the information given on birth, death, and marriage certificates taken together also provides valuable details that can open up many more avenues for your research. The recorded cause of death, for example, can lead you to local newspaper reports of the accident, obituaries, funeral home records, and cemetary records. And if you can't find the vital records you're looking for, family Bibles, school records, and military pension applications can be great substitutes.

Q **From the death indexes, I have the date of birth of my ancestor. But why can't I find the relevant entry for his birth?**

How did it go?

A *If, despite having the exact date of birth, you cannot find the entry that you are looking for, and you've checked the indexes immediately before and after that date, then you need to treat the information with some caution and broaden your search, working forward from the last known "sighting" of your ancestor. People often remember the birthday of relatives but not necessarily a year of birth or age. Your ancestor may have been one of the many who for various reasons changed their age, or there could have been an error in the transcription.*

Q **Why can't I find my ancestor in the indexes?**

A *The most common reason why you can't locate your ancestor is that the basic information you have is incorrect. How reliable is the information that you actually have? Just because it is in writing does not mean that the details are correct. Remember: any information is only as good as the person who gave it. My parents' marriage certificate contains several inaccuracies—information provided by my father. My father's name on the certificate is not the same as that on his birth certificate. It also states his father was deceased, which he wasn't—he died ten years after my parents married.*

8

Let no man put asunder

In the past, the best of intentions often ended in separation and divorce, though not as commonly as they do today.

Just as they do today, and for most of the same reasons, couples occasionally wanted to go their separate ways.

According to the National Marriage Project, a nonpartisan research group at Rutgers Univeristy, the rate of divorce in America has doubled since 1960, but has declined slightly since peaking in the 1980s. The probability of divorce hovers between 40 and 50 percent.

Though not as common in the old days, there is a chance that one of your ancestors called it quits with their better half, or maybe filed a petition but ended up staying married. A search through the county files may yield a record and new insights.

Historically, there have been two official kinds of divorce: absolute and limited. A limited divorce, or divorce *a mensa et thoro* ("from bed and board"), is more commonly known today as a separation. The parties are still married, but they no longer live together or enjoy the perks of being husband and wife. An absolute divorce, or

Here's an idea for you...

Discovering that there was a divorce, or more likely just a separation, in the family can be quite difficult as it is the sort of thing people don't tell the grandchildren, so tread carefully. This is an area where you need to be sure of your facts and you may have to be quite persistent when speaking to those older, living relatives. Look carefully at the census returns to see if there is a change of name, particularly for the "wife" for whom you cannot find any marriage to the "husband."

divorce *a vinculo matrimonii* ("from the chain of marriage") dissolves the marriage and renders both parties single.

In fact, many more couples petitioned for divorce than actually went through with it. This might be a lucky break for you, as the petition is where you'll find the most information. These documents usually include names of the spouses, the date or length of marriage, information on any children, and possibly details on any jointly held property. Unfortunately, early petitions can sometimes be hard to find. While you may find some indexed on the web, your best bet is to contact the vital records office of the state where your ancestor resided. You can also try searching the Family History Library's catalog (www.familysearch .org/eng/library/FHLC/frameset_fhlc.asp).

These days, divorces generate two different records in most states. The first is the divorce decree, which is a document prepared by the court in the jurisdiction where the divorcing parties live. This record will list the names of the parties involved, the date and location of the marriage, as well as the terms and any conditions of the divorce. This is usually filed with the county court.

More recently, states have also begun filing divorce certificates. These documents contain the same basic information as the decree, as well as details about where and when the marriage was dissolved. These records are on file with the state's Vital Records office, usually a division of the Department of Health. For purposes of confidentiality, some states have limitations on who may access or request these files. Other states, however, have online databases open for searching.

If you can't find an official record of an ancestor's divorce, you may want to check the archives of his local newspaper. It was not uncommon for a husband to take out a notice in the town's paper, announcing that he was no longer responsible for his wife or any bills she might incur. You can also look for clues in changing census data, omissions from or changes in wills and deeds, or wedding announcements a few years down the line. (Just don't forget that these changes can also indicate the death of a spouse.) If your family was well-known, you might even want to check the society column.

With partner-changing being far more prevalent than most people would have expected, the legitimacy of the children can sometimes be in doubt. Can genetic research help? See IDEA 36, *Wading into the gene pool*.

Try another idea...

"Divorce is like matrimony: a fellow has to go through it three or four times before he knows how."
EDGAR SALTUS (1855–1921), author

Defining idea...

"My first wife divorced me on the grounds of incompatibility, and besides, I think she hated me."
OSCAR LEVANT (1906–1972), pianist, composer, and wit

Defining idea...

How did
it go?

Q   I can't find any evidence that my several times great-grand-mother ever married her second "husband" and I know her first husband died after her. Yet she lived with this other man, took his surname, and had several children by him. Could this happen if she was not properly divorced from husband number one?

A   *Not only could it happen, but it sometimes did. The number of married individuals who moved in with another would have been hugely in excess of the number of legal, official divorces.*

Q   I know that a couple of my ancestors divorced in the twentieth century. Will I be able to find the reasons (because I'd really like to discover a bit of scandal in the family)?

A   *Some divorce certificates, petitions, and decrees will be more detailed than others—you may be able to find a juicy tidbit if you look closely. Most likely, though, the records will be all business.*

9

All the news that's fit to print

Newspapers are a fantastic resource for the local and family historian. They are full of information—both about people and places—that you will rarely find recorded anywhere else.

For hundreds of years, newspapers have been recording the news, both local and national. With obituaries, gossip columns, announcements, advertisements, sales particulars, and so forth, they were little different to those we know today.

On 24 April 1704, the first continuously published newspaper in the Colonies began by reprinting news from England and listing ship arrivals, birth and death notices, and accident reports.

Here's an idea for you... **If you have found something in a newspaper relating to an ancestor, don't stop there. Think about what follow-up stories or other records would have been generated by that event and search them out.**

From that point on, the newspaper industry began evolving to meet the needs of its readers. Big cities and towns often had daily papers, whereas smaller towns may have had weeklies. The small town locals contained more details, since everyone knew everyone and the focus was on what was going on in the community. Specialty newspapers also sprung up, catering to specific ethnic, religious, and trade groups.

Regardless of size or frequency, all papers traditionally included items of particular interest to genealogists:

- birth announcements
- wedding announcements
- obituaries
- community events
- classifieds
- advertisements

As the years went by, newspapers even began to offer pieces on engagements, accounts of recent weddings, anniversaries, and birthdays, and "in memoriams." Any of these items could offer up crucial details about the life of your ancestor. Wedding announcements and obituaries give the names and locations of relatives. Classifieds could reveal your family member selling property or goods.

Advertisements could memorialize your long-lost family business.

You shouldn't neglect the actual news in the newspaper, either. While your ancestor may not be mentioned directly, the stories will help you paint a picture of the times and community he lived in—not a hard and fast fact, but still an important part of understanding your history.

Newspapers outside the United States also played an important role in the emigration process, with the notices they carried providing information about the means of emigrating; information about the departure and arrival of ships; and the publication in advertisements of the names of local agents through whom passages might be arranged. Ships' notices also carried details of the availability of parcels of land that were on offer to prospective immigrants. Just as in the United States, many of these historical papers have been preserved and are available through libraries and national archives.

Due to the purposely disposable nature of newspapers and the fragility of the newsprint they were printed on, existence of and access to original publications is usually limited. Luckily, modern technology has allowed what does remain to be preserved on microfilm and electronic formats.

You could fully explore the myths and facts of some of those family stories by locating related newspaper items. Begin by looking at IDEA 2, *Who told you that?*

Try another idea…

"Were it left to me to decide whether we should have a government without newspapers, or newspapers without a government, I should not hesitate a moment to prefer the latter."
THOMAS JEFFERSON (1743–1826)

Defining idea…

Try free websites like Newspaper Abstracts (www.newspaperabstracts.com), or subscription-based sites (often available through your local history library) like Ancestry.com's newspaper collection (www.ancestry.com/search/rectype/ periodicals/news) or Newspaper Archive (www.newspaperarchive.com). The Family History Library also has a number of newspapers and obituaries available to search through their online catalog (www.familysearch.org/eng/library/FHLC/frameset_ fhlc.asp).

The Library of Congress also holds an extensive collection of historical newspapers, both on microfilm and electronically. Their collection stretches back to eighteenth-century American papers and some seventeenth-century foreign papers, even including some papers in their original printed formats. You can find a list of the LOC's holdings at www.loc.gov/rr/, most of which are available through interlibrary loan. Many local libraries have also made efforts to preserve newspapers from their communities.

What to do if the newspaper from your ancestor's area isn't indexed or available through online databases? It will take a bit more elbow grease, but dig in to the archives. To narrow your search, focus on issues printed around the time of your ancestor's birth, marriage, death, etc., and pay close attention to announcement sections, like the want ads, personals, and legal notices. Or, if your local history library subscribes, try searching for your ancestor in the indexes and abstracts available through the Periodical Source Index (PERSI) (www.heritagequestonline.com), which covers more than 6,000 journals dating from 1800.

Q **How can I get the best out of using newspapers?**

A *Unless you know the date of a specific event, searching newspapers can be very difficult. However, the national papers can provide priceless information about what was going on in the world at the time your ancestors lived, while local newspapers can tell you what was happening in the community. They can paint a detailed picture of the life and times of your ancestors in a way few other sources really can. Several commercial companies are now digitizing old newspapers and are in the process making them fully searchable. Indexes do exist for several national newspapers and are usually available in major libraries.*

Q **Where do I find copies of historical newspapers?**

A *Your local reference library should possess copies of any surviving local newspapers. Using the Internet, you should also be able to locate historical newspaper images, containing pictures from some of the most interesting events in more recent history. There are also a number of publications that list what is available and where. Facsimile copies of historical newspapers for specific dates are also available to purchase.*

How did it go?

10

Did he fall or was he pushed?

Our most intriguing ancestors are dead ones, particularly if their end was of the sticky variety. Coroners' reports and newspapers may reveal all.

The notion that our ancestors all died peacefully in their beds is, thankfully, a fallacy. Coming a close second to the miscreant ancestor in the popularity stakes is the one whose death was unusual—the more unusual the better.

If it isn't a family story passed down through the generations, then the first discovery that something untoward may have happened to an ancestor is often made when looking at the ordinary recording of his or her death. Death certificates have

Here's an idea for you...

Take another look at any death certificates you may have and see if in the "Informant" box there is any reference to the coroner or a coroner's inquest. A sudden, suspicious, or industrial death would probably involve the coroner. He could insist on a post-mortem examination and, in any case, provided the certificate for the body to be released and the death to be registered. Unless the death was really of major importance, it is probably only the local newspapers that would have covered the events, so concentrate on discovering where these are now held and seeing if they have the details you hope they have.

always given the cause of death—although too often it is something totally benign such as "Visitation of God" or "Old Age," or medical terms no longer used today. Far more gripping would be: Thomas Stevens died in 1891, "Accidentally killed by the fall of large mass from a stack of manure"—his last words can only be guessed at. And, in 1939, while enjoying a quiet walk along the beach, Mary Florence Savory died from "Crushing of the skull & evisceration of the brain due to being struck by the screw of an aeroplane after its crashing to earth." Cemetary and church burial registers though do not normally give such detailed, if any, information, except perhaps where the death was exceptional.

For more than one hundred years, individuals have been aiding law enforcement in investigating and determining causes of death in open cases. Depending on jurisdiction, these individuals are coroners or, more recently, medical examiners. The position of coroner comes from a centuries-old English tradition of electing a layperson (no medical degree required) to work in conjunction with doctors and law enforcement to provide cause of death information. Medical examiners are an American convention in which a physician with specialized training (often in law and/or forensics) is appointed to oversee and carry out medical investigations of certain deaths.

Though many of us now associate coroners and medical examiners with the violent homicides seen on *Law & Order*, their expertise is also required for suicides, deaths from poisoning, deaths in prisons, sudden or unexpected deaths, and any deaths in abnormal or suspicious circumstances. Coroners or medical examiners must also complete an inquest if there is a request to cremate the body of the deceased (though this is a more modern requirement).

Most deaths are going to be natural or accidental, but others may have involved a perpetrator who was subsequently brought to justice. See IDEA 33, *Crime and punishment*.

Try another idea...

"Don't go into Mr .McGregor's garden. Your Father had an accident there: He was put in a pie by Mrs. McGregor."
From *The Tale of Peter Rabbit* by
BEATRIX POTTER (1866–1943)

Defining idea...

Defining
idea...

"Murder, like talent, seems occasionally to run in families."
GEORGE HENRY LEWIS (1817–1878),
writer

Coroners' records may contain ancillary materials, including jury reports, pathology reports, and police reports. Generally, all materials attached to the coroners' reports and the reports themselves are considered public record and available for searching. These files can usually be found at the county level of the jurisdiction, though duplicate records may also exist on the city and state levels. Medical examiners can also issue death certificates, which list the name, sex, time and place of death, and the ruling on the cause and manner of death. Death certificates are available through each state's Vital Records office or the Department of Health. For more on using coroner's records in your genealogical research, check out *Your Guide to Cemetery Research* by Sharon Carmack.

Q **I'm supposed to have a great-grandfather who committed suicide by drowning himself in the local river. Would there be a record of that?**

How did it go?

A *The verdict from a coroner's inquest may be suicide or "deceased took his own life while of unsound mind." When suicide was taboo, many courts would have opted for the less condemnatory verdict or simply left it as open. So, when Elizabeth Adams drowned herself and her infant daughter in a stream in 1841, their death certificates both just give "drowned" as the cause of death although the mother's postnatal depression, almost certainly undiagnosed then, was probably the true cause.*

Q **My mother says her great-uncle was killed in "mysterious circumstances" during the early 1900s but I can't find any specific records about it. Any suggestions?**

A *Newspapers are often the only source of detailed information that can flesh out the often bland and enigmatic entry on a death certificate or in a burial register. See what you can find there.*

11

Writ in stone

Slabs, grave markers, headstones, memorial gardens, crematoria, and churchyards can all bring the dead back to life for you—metaphorically speaking, that is.

"Here lies the remains of James Paddy, brickmaker, late of this parish, in the hope that his clay will be re-molded in a workmanlike manner far superior to his former perishable materials."

"Monument inscription" is a term used for anything that is engraved or written on any type of memorial, from gravestones in a graveyard to massive monuments. These are an invaluable source of information for family and local historians alike, as in the example above—though not always as complimentary as they could be.

Some early inscribed memorials are found within the churches themselves, installed by the wealthier inhabitants of the parish. These memorials can take the form of effigies, monuments, memorial brasses, windows, benefactors' boards, vases, pews, organs, lecterns, or communion plates, all of which may have inscriptions. In the churchyard, graves were originally either unmarked or occasionally marked with a rock, boulder, or wooden cross, which eventually rotted away.

The better-off marked their place of burial with gravestones. What gravestones there were did not always survive.

Monument inscriptions usually include the dates of death and birth, and may also outline relationships and give an occupation (either as text or emblems, such as tools of the trade used by the deceased). In addition, monument inscriptions can carry a hidden message (although occasionally it is forthright, as in the James Paddy example). Evidence of migration or immigration may also be revealed.

If you're descended from European royalty, there may be a coat of arms on the grave. Although few families were armigerous, a coat of arms on a memorial can help distinguish the family from others of the same name. In the UK, the College of Arms was responsible for the supervision of the funerals of armigers, as well as the use of arms and epitaphs on monuments, and also issued funeral certificates. These are a rich source of family information and can describe not only the deceased but also provide information on the extended family.

With luck you can easily construct a substantial family tree from a single monument. Finding a mother, father, and children buried together and all appearing on the gravestone is not unusual. Even the simplest inscription can fill a gap in your family tree and help prove the relationship between two individuals. It is not uncommon to find several family graves grouped together in a cemetary. Most kept burial registers for their burial grounds. Monument inscriptions can therefore be a vital record for researching ancestors.

Here's an idea for you...

Include photographs of your families' gravestones in your family history file. It will create interest and may be the only "visible presence" your ancestor has.

Memorials to those cremated may be found in a columbarium or elsewhere nearby. These can take the form of plaques on walls or monuments, or on plaques dedicating rose bushes, trees, benches, etc. Ashes may be buried in the consecrated ground of a church-yard. In this case there should not only be an entry in the parish burial register, but possibly also a monument inscription in the church-yard itself.

For centuries, antiquarians and historians have transcribed and recorded monument inscriptions, resulting in the survival of inscriptions from graveyards that "disappeared" long ago. More recently this has been undertaken by genealogical societies. Most of these have been published and may be available for purchase. Otherwise, copies can often be found at the local archives or transcribed online. Sharon Carmack's *Your Guide to Cemetary Research* is a great source for more information.

Just because a name appears on a gravestone does not mean that that person was buried there. Check the burial register to confirm who is actually buried there. This is especially important with memorials within churches, which often refer to those buried elsewhere. See IDEA 22, *Open the doors and see the people.*

Try another idea…

"If a man needs an elaborate tombstone in order to remain in the memory of his country, it is clear that his living at all was an act of absolute superfluity."
OSCAR WILDE (1854–1900)

Defining idea…

How did it go?

Q   **I've been extremely fortunate in discovering what appears to be a very early and detailed family gravestone. However, its condition looks too good to be true. Should I trust it?**

A   *You are right to be suspicious. Tombstones with what appear to be very early dates should be treated with caution because information was often inscribed retrospectively—that is, a stone erected for one generation could have details of the parents included at the same time. Hence, the ages and dates are very possibly inaccurate. Careful examination of the inscription may reveal that a number of burials were recorded only when the most recent burial occurred, the giveaway being that all of the inscription itself has obviously been cut at the same time.*

Q   **I have discovered that an ancestor was buried in a large grave-yard. Unfortunately the stone is gone and the monument inscriptions have not been recorded. How can I discover exactly where my ancestor was laid to rest and if there is any surviving information?**

A   *It's not as difficult as you might think. There will almost certainly be a plan of the graveyard or churchyard and/or interments register, both of which will have references to grave numbers. Often these can be found either with the local cemetary or church authority, or deposited at the local county record office/library.*

12

Reading, 'riting, 'rithmetic

Education records are an excellent and often overlooked source of family and local history.

Not only can they give you information about a child's formative years, but also factual information about the whole family and the community in which they were placed.

Public schools have long been a part of American society. So long, in fact, that the Massachusetts Bay Colony established its first school in 1643, long before the United States of America was established. Education has been an important issue for the American people since those earliest days, though the push for public primary education didn't begin in earnest until after the Revolutionary War. By 1870, all states supplied free elementary schooling for children.

Just as they do today, early educational institutions kept a number of records on students and their families. These records can reveal a wealth of information to help you on your genealogical quest.

If you know the school your ancestor attended, and if it is still operational, contact the school directly about obtaining your family member's records. Though more modern records may be subject to privacy restrictions, obtaining older records can be significantly easier. If your ancestor's school has closed since he attended, contact the county's board of education to see if the records have been archived.

Of the records you may come across, registration data could be the most helpful. When a student enrolls in school, his parents or guardian must furnish pertinent details, including the full name of the child, his date of birth, the names of the parents, address of residence, and other contact information. Medical histroy details may even be included.

In order to put together a more rounded picture of your ancestor, you may be interested in digging up his report cards or transcripts. Grade reports for schoolchildren should be kept on file at the school, or in the event of its closing, with the board of education. For institutions of higher education, contact the registrar's office of the college or university. These reports will give you some insight into your ancestor's aptitude in school, as well as some hints about her talents and interests.

Here's an idea for you... **Many schools have long since celebrated their centennials. Take a look in the local reference library or archives to see if a history has been written about the schools that you are interested in.**

You should also inquire about copies of old school yearbooks, or visit the library in the area of your family member's school. Many times, libraries will have copies of school yearbooks or annuals in their local history sections. Though high schools and colleges have traditionally produced yearbooks, there has been a trend toward including elementary and middle schools in the practice as well. If you're lucky enough to locate your ancestor in multiple books, you'll be able to track her physical changes over the years, and learn precious details about extracurricular activities and friends.

To see a school through the eyes of its earlier scholars, explore IDEA 48, *A rue with a view*. See if you can discover any contemporary postcards of it.

Try another idea...

Alumni records could also hold valuable information. Colleges and universities often keep detailed and extensive records on the individuals who have passed through their gates, and many schools have entire offices dedicated to staying in touch with former students. Direct your inquiries to the alumni office, or visit the school's website to see if alumni information is available online.

"Education is a wonderful thing, provided you always remember that nothing worth knowing can ever be taught."
OSCAR WILDE (1854–1900)

Defining idea...

How did it go? **Q   Why did it take until 1870 for schooling to become compulsory?**

A   *There was a strong belief in earlier times that education of the working classes was unnecessary. They only needed skills for the job for which they were destined; also, if children spent time in school, a source of cheap labor would be lost. Others thought that educating the masses would lead to increases in vice and crime and also render them insolent to their superiors.*

Q   Where will I find school records?

A   *Information on schools and their records can be found in a variety of places, including local archives, local education authorities, libraries, and at the schools themselves. British census records will give information on staff and children at residential schools; however, American censuses list boarding school students at their parental home and college students are counted where they go to school. Also, local libraries may have back copies of newspapers with stories about a school.*

13

The sense of the census

One of the most important—and easily accessible—primary resources for local and family historians is the census. Learning how to interpret it properly will pay handsome dividends.

The census records offer a snapshot in time providing details of a specific family.

Census records can be used not only to further your search for ancestors, but also to broaden your knowledge of the wider family or your community, supplementing information found in other sources. Geographic mobility can be easily tracked through the given birthplaces, and social mobility through addresses and occupations.

THE ORIGINS

It is extremely important to remember why these records were generated—which was not for any of us to research our family or local history. These records can be difficult to navigate. A specialized guide, like Kathleen W. Hinckley's *Your Guide to the Federal Census,* may be helpful as you begin your research.

The first federal census was conducted in 1790 and subsequent censuses have been taken every ten years since. Because of their steady, consistent collection, census records offer genealogists a wonderful place to start searching for ancestors and tracking their lives and movements over time. It is important to note, however, that privacy laws prohibit the release of census data for 72 years after its collection, so the 1930 census is the most recent available for searching.

Here's an idea for you... **The National Archives have census data on archive and available to the public from 1790 to 1930. Much of this information has been digitized and may be available on the Internet. It is best to start your search with the 1930 census and work backward.**

The census has evolved with the needs of the country, making each collection slightly different than the one before. Here are some general descriptions of what you'll find in each set of records:

1790 Census: The first of the censuses was basically an early effort to determine the number of people living in the United States. Marshals were instructed to visit each household and list whomever lived there. Inhabitants were categorized by age and sex: free white males over 16, free white males under 16, free white females, and slaves. Only the head of the household was listed by name.

1800 and 1810 Censuses: The second and third censuses contain much the same information as the 1790 census, but the data is slightly more refined. Though the head of the family is still the only person listed by name, all other free members of the household are listed in more defined age brackets: younger than 10, 10 to 16, 16 to 26, 26 to 45, and 45 and older. Other free people and slaves living in the house are tallied as well.

1820 and 1830 Censuses: The fourth census refines the age groupings further, adding the 16 to 18 category for free white males. This census also contains information on occupations and members of the household who were not naturalized. The fifth census again refines information on ages of inhabitants, breaking the categories down to brackets of five years: 0 to 5, 5 to 10, etc. Categories for "deaf, blind, and dumb" and alien persons were also added, as were categories for free "colored" heads of household.

1840 Census: The sixth census included several very important additions. This census was the first to record ages of Revolutionary War pensioners. This column is particularly significant because pensioners were not necessarily the veterans themselves; widows and other dependents were often the beneficiaries of the pensions. This census also gathered information on occupations, as well as the number of persons in school, the number of illiterate persons over the age of 21, and the number of "insane."

1850 Census: The seventh census is often referred to as the first modern census, as it was the first census in which every member of the household is named (with the exception of slaves). Further additions included categories for birthplace, value of any property, whether married during the year, whether attended school during the year, literacy, and whether any persons were "idiotic" or "convicts." This census was also the first to come with instructions for completion, and required that copies of the records be filed with county, state, and federal authorities.

1860 and 1870 Censuses: The 1860 census added data on personal property value, and the 1870 census included columns for Mother Foreign Born and Father Foreign Born.

1880 Census: The tenth census included a new column for the birthplace of the father and mother, as well as the extremely important column for each persons' relationship to the head of the household. Information on marital status was also included. Residents of urban areas were asked to provide house numbers and street names for their homes.

1890 Census: The vast majority of this census was destroyed by fire. There was a special census of Union soldiers taken that year, however, which remains partially intact.

Use clues from the census to find birth, marriage, and death records, giving you more personal information and opening up other avenues for research. See IDEA 7, *Hatches, matches, and dispatches.*

Try another idea...

"The true test of a civilization is not the census, nor the size of the cities, nor the crops— no, but the kind of man the country turns out."
RALPH WALDO EMERSON (1803– 1882), poet and essayist

Defining idea...

1900–1930 Censuses: The 1900 census added month and year of birth for each person. The 1910 census indicated whether males were Union or Confederate soldiers. The 1920 and 1930 censuses include information on immigration and naturalization, as well as veteran status.

Though it is tempting to take the information found in census reports as hard facts, you have to remember that human error abounds in these reports. Memories can be faulty and mistakes could have been made in transcription. Use the census to start your investigation, and then keep digging.

How did it go?

Q Why can't I find my ancestor on the census?

A *If you are searching online using one of the indexes with links to the actual census images, it may be that the entry you are looking for has been incorrectly indexed or transcribed, or the name misspelled by the enumerator. If you think this is the case, be creative in your searches and try all spelling variations. Additionally, your ancestor may not have been present in the household on census night, and so might have been enumerated elsewhere or may have been missed by the enumerator. Also, a few census returns have not survived. If after a thorough search using the Internet you still can't find them and you know roughly where they lived, it may be worth doing an area search either online or by using microfilm copies of the actual returns at the National Archives.*

Q I've checked the 1870 and 1880 census for my ancestors but a different place of birth is given in each. How can that be?

A *It's very important to check and record the details given for your ancestors on every census. Places of birth may vary slightly due to boundary changes, places being renamed, or because your ancestors did not know exactly where they were born or they were more specific in one census than in another. Generally speaking, the nearer the person was living to their place of birth, the more precise the entry is likely to be.*

14

Location, location, location

Just as now, in previous centuries anyone wanting to know the location of a local plumber or undertaker, or even the address of an acquaintance, would turn to a local directory. You can turn those same pages.

In the pages of these now historic volumes are the names and addresses of the tradesmen and residents of yesteryear—your family and forebears or the lifeblood of the community in which you now reside.

The first recognizable directories made their appearance in large cities as early as the 1700s, with many cities publishing yearly directories in the 1800s. Most were chiefly concerned with listing traders and merchants.

The idea of directories developed over the following decades, coming to include residential information for all area families. Like the census, directories were generally compiled by a door-to-door canvass of the community, and often included spouse's name and information on occupation. Small towns were usually included

Here's an idea for you...

Although directories do have their limitations, they can give considerable information about a place and can be used as a starting point for research, or as a cross-reference to other sources, such as the census. Find a local directory for the place in which you now live and, for any particular year, build up a picture of the community or even just a few streets. Follow through from year to year, and you can trace the development of one area, or one street, from its first appearance, showing changes in use of any one building or premises over the years. Try checking the history of your house, beginning with its first appearance in the streets section and then the names of previous occupants can be tracked year by year.

in larger volumes covering entire counties, but may have begun producing their own directories as the population grew.

Directories are usually kept on the local level, with many copies being housed in libraries or historical archives. If the town in question does not have its own repository, it is worth combing though the Library of Congress's extensive collection of historic directories. Among the LOC's collection are:

- City and state directories up to and including 1860 on microfiche
- City and state directories from 1861 through 1960 on microfilm
- City and state directories from a huge range of years in their original paper formats
- Telephone directories on paper and microfilm

- Reverse telephone directories (also called street address or "criss-cross" directories)
- Selected Canadian and European city and telephone directories
- A complete listing of the LOC's holdings can be found at the Library itself or at http://catalog.loc.gov/.

Aside from the obvious details on names, addresses, and occupations, directories can provide plenty of other useful information. Take a look at the families who lived next door or down the street from your ancestors. Are their descendents still in the area? If so, try contacting them to see if they might remember anything about your family—long-forgotten personal anecdotes or photos that include your family member.

Don't forget to peruse the business listings in the directories as well. If you know your ancestor was a baker or a lawyer, look for advertisements for these services. You may find an ad placed by your great-great uncle—or perhaps his competitor!

Directories are not the only place where you can find lists of residents in a particular place. See IDEA 15, *Votes and voters*, to learn about electoral registers.

Try another idea...

"Obscenity can be found in every book except the telephone directory."
GEORGE BERNARD SHAW
(1856–1950)

Defining idea...

61

How did it go?

Q   **Looking though a 1910 directory, I was disappointed to find that number 27 was missing from the road where my family used to live. I know from a birth certificate that it was the family home in 1908 and the numbers on either side—25 and 29—were in the directory so 27 must have been there because all the houses would have been built at the same time. Why would this be?**

A   *As more directories were produced, people often became annoyed at being continually pestered for information, with the consequence that they did not respond to the agents' enquiries. Try looking for other directories, either a few years before or after 1910 or perhaps published by another company, as these may include the information you are looking for.*

Q   **An eccentric great-uncle of mine swears he unwittingly moved into a house that was once the scene of a bloody crime of passion, but he refuses to say more. Even my parents don't know if he's serious. How can I call his bluff?**

A   *If you know the address and you can find the relevant local directories going back year to year, you'll be able to track the owners or occupants of the house. Cross-referencing those names and dates with stories in the local papers should give you the answers you're looking for.*

15

Votes and voters

Although not all of us were able to vote until 1924, if you know who could vote, where, and when, then another potential source of information about your ancestors becomes available.

As with many historical records, getting the best from electoral records requires a little knowledge about their background: why and when they were generated and, specifically, what the qualifications were to vote, as these changed with changing legislation.

The right to participate in the democratic process has been a battle hard-won in this country. Though the Constitution now guarantees all citizens over the age of eighteen, regardless of sex or race, the right to vote, it was not always so.

Here's an idea for you... **Locating where someone was living during the twentieth century can be difficult. Try finding any relevant birth, death, or marriage certificates. This will give you an address to check against the electoral registers for your ancestors.**

AFRICAN-AMERICANS

The Fifteenth Amendment to the Constitution, ratified in 1870, decreed that the right to vote could not be denied to any citizen "on account of race, color, or previous condition of servitude." This amendment provided former slaves the ability to cast their ballots. Though African-Americans were legally eligible to vote, several hurdles prevented them from doing so. In many Southern states, a potential voter had to first pass a literacy test. Passing the exam was virtually impossible, given the high rate of illiteracy at the time, as well as the prejudiced judging of the tests. African-Americans were also subject to a biased poll tax as a prerequisite to voting, which many individuals were not able to pay. Aside from these practices, African-American voters were also subjected to various forms of intimidation and discrimination. The passage of the Twenty-fourth Amendment in 1964 banned poll taxes, and the National Voting Rights Act of 1965 banned the use of literacy tests.

WOMEN

Although American women were a great political force behind the abolitionist and prohibitionist movements in the United States, they were denied eligibility to vote in federal elections until 1920. The ratification of the Nineteenth Amendment ensured that "the right of citizens in the United States to vote shall not be denied or abridged by the United States or by any State on account of sex."

YOUNG ADULTS

As national controversy over America's involvement in the Vietnam War raged in 1968, pressure to lower the voting age from 21 to 18 intensified. Many people found a supreme injustice in the fact that 18-year-olds could be drafted into military service but could not participate in the election of the government that sent them to war. In response to national outcry, the Twenty-sixth Amendment was introduced, stating that "the right of citizens of the United States, who are eighteen years of age or older, to vote shall not be denied or abridged by the United States or by any State on account of age"; it was instituted in 1971.

VOTER REGISTRATION RECORDS

The records you find will vary in content over time and from state to state. Generally, though, some standard information will appear:

Full name
Date of birth
Gender
Address
Naturalization

Older records may also include a physical description, marital status, and detailed citizenship information. More modern records will include phone numbers and party affiliation. These details will suggest more resources to explore, like city directories and local newspapers' coverage of political affairs. They will also add to your mental picture of your relatives as you learn about their political views and participation in the electoral process.

"Vote early and vote often."
AL CAPONE (1899–1947)

Defining idea...

67

How did it go?

Q **Where will I find voter registration records?**

A *Voter registration records can often be found on the county level, though each state has different rules on accessing them. Some states, like California, have made efforts to make their historical voter information available online, while other states' records remain sealed. Contact your local library or county election authority for information on the records you're seeking.*

16

Taxing the community

Taxation is as old as time, and that's just as well from the historians' perspective because tax records offer a wealth of information about the lives of our ancestors.

The Greeks and Romans complained about taxation. Jesus was born in a stable in Bethlehem because Mary and Joseph were traveling to register for taxation. Lady Godiva rode naked through the streets of Coventry to induce her husband to abolish local taxation.

Over the years, the government applied taxes to just about anything and everything, in an attempt to raise revenue to fund their activities. As they did so, complex systems of record keeping evolved.

Many of the early tax records give extensive lists of names, providing us with early "census" substitutes. Not only can they give you information about an individual but also about relationships. They also give actual addresses and details about property. This can include the individuals' houses, farms, boats, and carriages, painting a glorious picture of the way they lived and fit into their community.

Just as they are today, historical taxes were complex and varied. And, as Americans found with the institution of the Internal Revenue Act in 1862, just about everything and everyone was subject to them. Income taxes, licensing fees, poll taxes, property (real and personal) taxes, stamp taxes, and a multitude of duties were imposed in every state and territory in the union. Bad for your ancestors, but good for you, because the records left behind can help you trace their footsteps.

County tax rolls are a good place to start your search. Dating from the 1700s to the late nineteenth century, these records will offer plenty of useful information, including the name of the head of household, details on the property being taxed, and other potentially useful tidbits. These records are fairly easy to find and search through the county courthouse or local archives, and many microfilmed records are available through the Family History Library (www.familysearch.org/eng/library/FHLC/frameset_fhlc.asp).

Income tax records, which will contain the name, address, and occupation of every gainfully employed individual subject to the tax law, will provide much of the same material as early census reports. Unlike census reports, however, tax data was collected every year. Following your ancestor through consecutive records will help you pinpoint important events in his life—moving to or from an area, taking a new job, receiving an inheritance.

Ancestors who owned land or homes were liable for real property taxes. These records can also be revealing, as they will show names, addresses, and pertinent information about

Here's an idea for you...

Many archives now have a searchable catalog—sometimes even available online. Check out just what taxation records have survived for your areas of interest. You may even find a pro forma "tax certificate" for one of your ancestors.

the property, like its location, size, usage, and value. Even individuals with no land were subject to taxes on personal property; pianos, pleasure carriages, and watches were all fair game. All these details can give you hints about your ancestors' lifestyles and habits.

The government also required professionals in a number of fields to renew an annual license of practice—for a small fee, of course. Doctors, bankers, hotel owners—everyone owed the government something. Even the ladies had to pay stamp taxes on their cosmetics.

Though income tax records from the Civil War period will be hard to come by, as they were burned after the income tax was declared unconstitutional, the National Archives and Record Administration (NARA) is currently spearheading an effort to collect and preserve the surviving assessment lists created during that period. These lists, which detail information about monies collected from businesses and their corresponding licenses, are available on microfilm and are searchable on the NARA website (www.archives.gov).

Those you think should have left wills often didn't, and those that you think wouldn't often did. To investigate what your ancestor was really worth, start by looking at IDEA 23, *Where there's a will.*

Try another idea...

"The avoidance of taxes is the only intellectual pursuit that still carries any reward."
JOHN MAYNARD KEYNES
(1883–1946)

Defining idea...

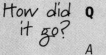

Q   **So how do I access some of these taxation records?**

A   *In the United States tax records were kept at the local level and may be found in local libraries.*

17

How does the land lie?

Maps and plans are a cornucopia of landscape information. Plot the geographical changes in your community and see how it grows.

Our environment is constantly changing as ancient historic sites disappear: woodland, farms, whole villages come and go. Even in towns, historic terraces are replaced by modern McMansions and superstores.

The significance of maps and plans does not stop with raw landscape information, because those changes in the landscape came about because of historical and social change. Hence, their value in providing a series of contemporaneous snapshots detailing features created before the date of the survey cannot be overemphasized. Much of the detailed information will depend on the scale used but all maps and plans are valuable sources for researching the evolution of a street, farm, estate, village, or town.

Here's an idea for you... **To see how useful and informative maps and plans can be, and how relatively easy they are to use, pick somewhere you are interested in and just see what maps and plans your local record office has for that place and what period they cover. Scan the Internet, too, where you will find several websites that include digitized old maps, as well as current maps and even aerial photographs.**

Land has always been an important element of the American culture—exploring it, claiming it, transforming it (for better or worse). Luckily for genealogists, this preoccupation resulted in extensive mapping. Here are some resources for finding your ancestors' little corner of the world.

LOCAL LIBRARIES, ARCHIVES, COURT HOUSES

Because maps play such a significant role in the day-to-day functioning of a community—defining school districts, property lines, voting districts—they are often carefully preserved on the local level. Check with the library in your ancestor's town to see what maps are available for searching. You might also be directed to other facilities, like universities or historical societies, that hold different, specialized maps.

US GEOLOGICAL SURVEY

Established in 1879, the USGS is responsible for classifying and mapping land in the United States. Their archives hold microfilm of maps dating back to the organization's earliest days and hard copies of current maps. Reproductions of their holdings are available for a small fee. Simply contact the USGS with the details of your search—

Defining idea... *"God made the country, and man made the town."*
WILLIAM COWPER (1731–1800),
The Task

74

location, time frame, any particular points of interest, like farms over 100 acres, say—and a researcher will determine the best map for you.

The Land Ordinance Act has definitive maps associated with it. Find out more in IDEA 42, *The Land Ordinance Act*.

Try another idea…

THE NATIONAL ARCHIVES

About 900 historical maps are held in the National Archives and Record Administration (NARA), dating from the late eighteenth century to the early 1920s. Drawn from a variety of sources, these maps generally outline states and territories rather than cities or towns. You can search the holdings at www.archives.gov/publications/finding-aids/maps/, or you can examine the maps directly in person. Reproductions can be ordered through the Archives website.

THE LIBRARY OF CONGRESS

The LOC is home to some 5 million maps, a significant portion of which are maps of US counties and states. Most of these maps date back to the nineteenth century, and include the extensive collections from the eras of colonialism, the Revolutionary War, the War of 1812, the Civil War, and World Wars I and II. The LOC's holdings are open to the public, and research librarians are always available to help. The catalog can also be searched online at http://catalog.loc.gov/.

For more land records, see Patricia Law Hatcher's *Locating Your Roots*. Maps are covered in detail in *The Family Tree Resource Book for Genealogists* and *The Red Book*.

"Maps encourage boldness. They're like cryptic love letters. They make anything seem possible."
MARK JENKINS, travel columnist and writer, *To Timbuktu*

Defining idea…

75

How did it go?

Q **I managed to get ahold of some wonderful old maps at a garage sale that show the area where I live before the developers moved in. I'd really like to know what was there before the 1930s, which is the date of the oldest map I've found. The local studies department at my library does have some early maps but nothing earlier than mine. What can I do?**

A *Make a trip to your local county record office, where they will probably have all sorts of plans, such as estate plans, sales particulars for the big estates, and perhaps plans attached to deeds and mortgages from very early times. Some record offices have their catalog available online so you can make some investigations before you go.*

Q **I have quite a few maps of my area going back a long way but it's very difficult to follow all the development because they're in so many different forms and scales. Any suggestions as to how I could clarify my collection?**

A *Try to download digitized copies of what you've already got, and any other missing pieces of the puzzle. If you have the skills and the equipment, scan the hard copies into your computer. Then, adjust the scales of the maps on screen so they're all the same. You can then produce a series of overlays so you can see very clearly how change and development took place. It's really not as difficult as it may sound ... honest!*

18

Become a where wolf

Begin your prowl and discover what's found where within the giant labyrinth of archives, libraries, and record repositories.

Though the United States may be a young country compared to other nations in the world, we have a dynamic and complex history. Many of the documents recording that history are yours for the searching if you know where to look.

For anyone interested in their own past or in their country's heritage, there are immensely rich veins of information to be unearthed. The National Archives and Record Administration (NARA), based in Washington, DC, has one of the largest archival collections in the world, spanning more than 200 years of American history, from the earliest census to federal documents recently released to the public.

Here's an idea for you... **Make a visit to your local record offices. They can cover the whole spectrum of family and local history, and their experienced staff will guide you to deeds, maps, photographs, possibly copies of local census returns, and much else. You'll be amazed what you can discover. Make sure you check the opening times before you go though.**

The NARA was created in 1934 to serve as a central repository for the records of federal government agencies. Before the Archives were created, each agency was responsible for the storage and maintenance of its own records. Naturally, the degree of care with which these records were kept varied from agency to agency. As the first archivists discovered when they began collecting documents for archiving, many important materials had suffered extensive damage from age, fire, water, even insects and animals. The NARA has taken extensive and exhaustive measures to restore and preserve such materials, and their collection methods today ensure that all documents stored under their purview are maintained meticulously.

Among the NARA records available are:

- Federal population census records
- Military records
- Immigration records and ships' passengers lists
- Naturalization records
- Federal land records
- Internal Revenue Service assessment lists
- Patents records
- Federal court records
- Maps

Other important collections of records include those held in the Library of Congress (LOC), the world's largest library. Established in 1800, the LOC is the research branch of the United States Congress and today boasts more than a million items and 530 miles of shelves. Within its extensive holdings you will find:

- Manuscripts
- Photographs
- Newspapers
- Maps
- Vertical files for various families, states, towns, and cities

Important and useful as the NARA and the LOC are, many, if not most, of the records you require are held at the local level. Every county has its own record office and nearly every town has its own library. It is in these locations that you will find records created by local authorities, business papers, electoral records, court records, school records, photographs, maps, local newspapers, and even private collections of papers and letters.

The diversity of American documentary heritage means that anyone who wants to delve into their past, to research their ancestry or the history of their home, village, or town, is guaranteed an abundance of riches. Start your search at the online catalogs of the NARA at www.archives.gov.

If your research suggests your family underwent a major upheaval at some point, the local paper at that time might shed more light on the reasons. Check out IDEA 9, *All the news that's fit to print*.

Try another idea...

"History: An account mostly false, of events unimportant, which are brought about by rulers mostly knaves, and soldiers mostly fools."
AMBROSE BIERCE (1842–1914), short story writer and journalist

Defining idea...

How did
it go?

Q   **I'm a bit overwhelmed by the number of possible archives, libraries, and record offices that may have what I want—or may not. Is there a way of finding which are going to be the most likely to be able help me with my search for my roots? I don't have the time to visit them all.**

A   *Yet again the World Wide Web comes to our rescue. Nearly every major archive—national, local, or private—has its own website detailing its hold-ings. The NARA website contains a wealth of information, not only on its own collections. Through this website, there is access to many hundreds of other record offices and archives, to listings of their holdings, and to their contact details. It's a veritable Pandora's box of goodies.*

Q   **I've been told that I cannot see some records because they are "closed." What does that mean?**

A   *The Freedom of Information Act came into effect in 1966, giving the right of access to information held by many public bodies. Some records, though, for very good reasons, do remain with a statutory closure period in force. The record office should be able to give you specific information and there is guidance on the National Archives website.*

19

Files, formats, and family trees

Clarity, convenience, and completeness are the golden rules for organizing your research. Living by them might be difficult, but the benefits are well worth the effort.

If cleanliness is next to godliness, then neatness cannot be far behind.

I have a closet. It houses the results of my many years of research into my past. It is organized in a series of neat binders, uniformly labeled and color-coded. The pages within are all neatly typed with the pages cross-referenced. Everything is easy to find and I am proud of my collection. I am dreaming.

It is so very easy to become absorbed in your research with little realization of the need to record your findings systematically, thoroughly, and carefully, and to then file them in such a way that they can be easily recovered and used by you and those who will come after you. So what do you need to consider?

Here's an idea for you… **You can find all manner of blank forms into which to enter the results of your research online. But why not design your own? Apart from being considerably cheaper, they can be customized to suit your filing system and your personal needs.**

ONE—BEFORE YOU BEGIN

Where am I? Which library? What record office? What is the date? What am I looking for? Great-Aunt Matilda who? Do I have a headache or have I left my reading glasses at home?

TWO—THE RECORD

What am I looking at? Is it a book, microfilm, an original, a website? Does it have a title? What is its reference number? Is it a transcript, abstract, extract, or something else that may be incomplete? Are there missing pages, torn pages, gaps in the record? How easy is it for me to read? Easy as pie: It's in Latin, and it was written by an arthritic monk!

THREE—THE SEARCH

What/who am I looking for? Am I searching the whole thing or just part of it—specific time period, particular chapter, only the index? Am I looking for all occurrences of a surname or place or only for a very specific event? What variants, if any, of the name am I looking for?

FOUR—TAKING DOWN THE INFORMATION

What did I not find? This is just as important to note as what you did find, because you do not want to waste time in the future not finding it for a second time.

One of the best ways to copy information is to take a photograph of it, so see IDEA 49, *Cameras are not just for vacations!*

Try another idea…

Transcribe everything exactly. Do not abbreviate and do not expand—"Mgt." Brown stays as "Mgt." so don't write down "Margaret" because it might have been "Mry." "Buckinghamshire" stays as just that and not "Bucks" or in six years' time you will read it as "Berks." Note down any omissions or gaps. If you can't read something or are unsure of a word or two, then write yourself a note that says so; or speak nicely to a member of staff who may be able to help you.

There is a certain law that says you will find what you want just as the librarian announces, "We are closing in five minutes." There is every temptation to rush to get something finished. In fact there is always the temptation to get everything down as quickly as possible so you can get on to the next item. Not a good idea, as from such eagerness mistakes arise. Take deep breaths and slow down. The books, films, records will be there tomorrow—they have nowhere else to go.

"Exactness and neatness in moderation is a virtue, but carried to extremes narrows the mind."
FRANCOIS DE SALIGNAC FENELON
(1651–1715), French theologian
and author

Defining idea…

85

Nearly all libraries, record offices, and the like allow you to use laptops and PDAs—although you should ask first—but if you are a two-finger typist then errors when inputting will undoubtedly happen. It is therefore doubly important that you check very carefully what you have entered before you go home.

FIVE—AT HOME

Try to analyze your findings as soon as you can, while your recent discoveries are still clear in your mind, because then you will realize any failings in your note-taking. Come up with a system of filing and storing that suits *you*. There is no right way, although there are several things you do need to consider. Consistency is the key word here. This covers areas such as size of paper, referencing systems, organization of the papers (by name, by family, by place, by date—whatever suits you). If you are using a computer program to record your information, much the same applies.

Always remember to back up. And not only if you are keeping everything on computer—a second copy of the results of your toils should always be kept in a separate location, just in case …

"Good order is the foundation of all things."
EDMUND BURKE (1729–1797)

Q   **I have found this really interesting deed that I know mentions one of my forebears—at least I think it is interesting but I can't really read it because of the awful old handwriting. What can I do?**

How did it go?

A   *See if you can get a photocopy of the deed and then apply a modicum of perseverance. You will certainly be able to make out a word or two and bear in mind that there are only 26 letters in the alphabet. You'll be surprised how soon you can build up further words and then whole sentences.*

Q   **That didn't go well at all. Any other ideas?**

A   *The UK National Archives website at www.nationalarchives.gov.uk has a whole section dedicated to paleography (reading old handwriting) and another to Latin. Here you can learn all the tricks in a really fun way and within no time at all you will become much more competent. Or join a family or local history society where other members will certainly be able to help you.*

20

Fancy a date?

All dates are not the same so it is important that you understand the old dating practices in order to date documents correctly.

Given that the "modern" Gregorian calendar was adopted by different countries at different times, it is vital to get the background on dates and learn how to determine when an event actually happened.

For hundreds of years, the Julian calendar that had been introduced in Rome in 46 BC was used all over the world. Each year officially ran from 25 March to 24 March. By 1751, the Julian calendar, which was based on a nominal "year" of 365 days plus an extra day every four years, was eleven days out of step with the Gregorian calendar. This error had first been recognized early in the sixteenth century, but it wasn't until 1582 that Pope Gregory XIII undertook to correct it. He decreed in a papal bull that the day following 4 October 1582 would be 15 October (hence, Gregorian calendar). To avoid the problem recurring, the rule for leap years was also changed such that centenary years that were not divisible by 400 were not leap years.

Here's an idea for you...

To discover which day of the week an event actually took place, consult a perpetual calendar. The calendar will show, for example, that 25 October 1760 was a Saturday.

States obedient to the pope adopted the Gregorian calendar immediately. These were Spain, Portugal, Italy, and France. Prussia, the Catholic States of Germany, Holland, and Flanders adopted it in 1583; Catholic parts of Switzerland in 1583–84; Poland in 1586; Hungary in 1587; the German and Netherlands Protestant states and Denmark in 1700; and Sweden in 1753.

An Act of Parliament, Lord Chesterfield's Act of 1751, finally replaced the Julian calendar with the Gregorian calendar in England and Wales, bringing them in line with the rest of Europe. The Act stated that 1 January should be the first day of the year. Thus 1750 commenced on 25 March and ended 24 March 1750/51, while 1751 commenced 25 March 1751 and ended on 31 December 1751. Christmas Day remained as 25 December, even though the true anniversary was now 6 January. The changes were to apply to all the dominions of the British Crown.

For the 170 years between the papal bull of Gregory XIII and 1752, the two calendars had been used side by side in Western Europe. Thus communication in Europe was prone to ambiguities as far as dates were concerned. Even within England, a year starting on 1 January (known as the historical year) was in general use for almanacs, etc., and 1 January had always been celebrated as New Year's Day. The year starting 25 March was called the civil or legal year, although the phrase "Old Style" was commonly used. These ambiguities are not just a problem for modern researchers; they were a contemporary problem for which contemporary solutions were required. Prior to 1752, dates between 1 January and 24 March each year were expressed, for example, as 1 February 1700–01, written to show that the date was 1 February 1700 in the old style but 1 February 1701 in the new style—an attempt to try and differentiate between the old and new calendar.

Ambiguities continued in Eastern Europe into the twentieth century. Russia and Turkey converted to the Gregorian calendar in 1918, Yugoslavia and Romania in 1919, and Greece in 1923. Thus the October Revolution "happened" in what was November and Christmas is celebrated in Russia in January, because the old calendar was used to determine the dates of religious festivals. Japan adopted the Gregorian calendar in 1872. China started to use the Gregorian calendar for official and business purposes in 1912, but the traditional Chinese lunar calendar continues to be used for most personal matters, such as the celebration of birthdays and festivals, including when to celebrate the Chinese New Year. Make sure to note this if your research heads overseas.

Using maps from a number of different dates, you can plot the geographical changes in your community and see how it grew and changed over time. See IDEA 17, *How does the land lie?*

Try another idea...

"Don't be fooled by the calendar. There are only as many days in the year as you make use of. One man gets only a week's value out of a year while another man gets a full year's value out of a week."
CHARLES DOW RICHARDS
(1879–1956),
politician

Defining idea...

91

How did
it go?

Q **My ancestors hailed from the UK, and I've come across "regnal years" in my research. What are they?**

A *Early parish registers and manorial and legal records were dated using regnal years. This type of dating system started with the date of accession of each sovereign. For example, George III became King on 25 October 1760, thus "3 George III" would refer to the third year of King George's reign and run from 25 October 1762 to 24 October 1763. There are exceptions to the rule, the main ones being King Charles II, whose reign was deemed to have commenced on his father's execution in 1649 and not when he actually sat on the throne after the restoration of the monarchy in 1660, and King George II, because of the changes to the calendar during his reign in 1752. The use of regnal years decreased over time and they are now rarely used.*

21

On the move

Follow the branches of your family's migrations—they may stretch farther and wider than you think.

One of the times of greatest population movement was during the Industrial Revolution.

Although historians may disagree over exactly when the Industrial Revolution began and ended, most consider it to have lasted from the mid-eighteenth century until the end of the nineteenth century. Whatever the view, the many new and interesting inventions and improvements to the transport infrastructure transformed America from a mainly rural to a more urban population. These times saw the development of factories and mills, canals and railways, and the demise of many of the rural cottage industries.

It is not surprising, therefore, to discover just how mobile our ancestors were. Although some families stayed within a relatively small area, many did not, gradually moving through the country, motivated by economic necessity, employment, or trade. Merchants and others involved in trading could move around the country to maintain their livelihoods.

An ancestor may appear in the records of one of the large cities, but how do you discover where he came from? Census returns, tax records, and city directories allow you to track your ancestors' movements during the latter half of the nineteenth century (and sometimes earlier) relatively easily with the use of the Internet. Census records will indicate place of birth.

The International Genealogical Index (IGI) produced by the Church of Jesus Christ of Latter-day Saints is an online database containing over 700 million entries, mainly baptisms and marriages, taken from worldwide sources. It can open up many new possibilities for you. Although it is not fully comprehensive, the IGI can be a fantastic "finding" aid. Most counties have a baptism or marriage index that may reveal the origins of an ancestor. Often, these have been compiled by family history societies. Visit the IGI at www.familysearch.org/eng/search/frameset_search .asp?PAGE=igi/search_IGI.asp&clear_form=true.

Here's an idea for you...

If you are struggling to locate an ancestor in a particular area before civil registration was introduced, double-check that you haven't overlooked any major indexes covering the county. You might find him or her there.

A person's will might disclose his or her place of origin, or it may refer to previous places of residence. The will may list legacies of land and property far away from where the person died, some of which may give a hint as to an origin. Title deeds to property can give evidence of an ancestor owning land in several locations, which may open up other avenues.

City and trade directories are useful for tracking the movements of tradespeople, while the records of freemen, guilds, or livery companies may reveal places not only where someone traded but also from where they came.

Other records worth consulting that may also give a place of birth include professional and employment records, military records, court records, school or university records, monument inscriptions, and newspaper obituaries or reports of crime.

These are just some of the sources that may help you with your research. However, once you find a potential candidate from one of these, you really do need to look for collaborating evidence. When using any index, be sure to seek out the original record from which the information was gathered—most of which can be found at a local record office—for confirmation, accuracy, and to make sure that nothing has been missed. *Westward Expansion: A History of the American Frontier* by Ray Allen Billington and *The Family Tree Problem Solver* by Marsha Hoffman Rising are other great sources to explore.

There is usually some veracity in any family story, but establishing which parts are true and which aren't can be a problem. For more on this see IDEA 3, *Show and tell*.

Try another idea...

"Curiosity is one of the most permanent and certain characteristics of a vigorous intellect."
SAMUEL JOHNSON (1709–1784), lexicographer, critic, and poet

Defining idea...

How did it go?

Q **I have located the baptism of an ancestor in a large city. How-ever, all his siblings were baptised elsewhere. Can you explain why?**

A *You need to step back and take a broad look at the extended family to see whether there was any family connection with the city. Did they own prop-erty there? What was the father's occupation? Could that have caused the family to move temporarily? Or were they just passing through? Often women returned "home" to their mothers to give birth—especially for a first child—so that may be worth looking at as well.*

Q **My ancestor has a fairly unusual surname and I can't find anyone else in the area with that surname. Why might that be?**

A *Have you checked to see if anyone is doing a one-name study of your sur-name—that is, collecting all references worldwide? If someone is doing such a study, they may have information about your ancestor and his origins. It is also worth checking if anyone else is researching the same family in the same or adjoining counties. They, too, may have useful information. Many family history societies also run an index for "strays." A stray is a recorded event in which a person is described in the source record as being from, or connected with, a place outside the area in which they normally lived or were born.*

22

Open the doors and see the people

For centuries, religious groups have kept registers of ceremonies, marriages, and burials. They can very effectively open up a window on the lives of our forebears.

When researching your ancestors, religious registers are of immense value, not just as a record of ceremonies, burials, and marriages, but also in giving you a tremendous insight into the social history of the area.

Historically, the standards of record keeping varied tremendously, depending on who was actually responsible for doing it, leading to considerable variation in the quality of the registers of different groups. Generally, the earlier the register, the less information will be recorded.

But there is still plenty to learn from even the most scanty record. Just finding one proves your ancestor—or at least his parents—were practicing, active members of a religious community, and also puts that family in a certain place at a certain time. It is important to note that the vast majority of information—records of rites and ceremonies, member registers, details specific to the community—is kept by individual centers of worship. If you know where your ancestor lived or what house of worship he belonged to, your first step should be contacting that institution.

In the interest of preserving the culture and history of their faithful, however, many religious groups now have central libraries or archives where historical documents can be perused. A few to note:

The American Jewish Archives: Created after the devastation of the Holocaust, the AJA seeks to preserve the history of Jewish people in America. Boasting more than ten million pages of material, the AJA is home to manuscripts, photos, and other genealogical records, all available for searching in person or online at www .americanjewisharchives.org/aja/index.html.

The American Baptist Historical Society: Holding a broad range of materials documenting the missionary efforts of American Baptists in the United States and abroad, the ABHS is the authority on Baptist history. Their library will be most helpful to genealogists whose ancestors served as ministers or missionaries. You can find them on the web at www.baptisthistory.us/.

The Archives of the Evangelical Lutheran Church in America: The ELCA Archives are a centralized collection of materials covering the Lutheran movement in the United States. A number of congregational histories and member lists are held by the ELCA, a search of which may point you to the specific congregation where documents concerning your ancestor are held. Visit www.elca.org/archives/ for more information.

There is more to life than just being born, married, or dying. To really bring someone to life, look at IDEA 16, *Taxing the community*, to discover what else your ancestors were up to.

Try another idea...

The General Commission on Archives and History of the United Methodist Church: This repository holds a wide range of materials on the history of the Methodist church in America. Mainly focused on literature concerning Methodism, it also holds some biographical and genealogical resources. The catalog can be found at www.gcah.org/inventory.htm.

"Life is so constructed that an event does not, cannot, will not, match the expectation."
CHARLOTTE BRONTE (1816–1855)

Defining idea...

The Church of Jesus Christ of Latter-day Saints: The Church of Jesus Christ archives house materials covering the history of the Mormon church in America, including manuscripts, photos, oral histories, and fascinating details on Mormon Westward pioneer movement. The collection is extensively cataloged and indexed for easy searching. You can find links to each archive's catalog at www.lds.org/churchhistory/content/0,15757,3957-1-2117,00.html.

Additionally, the Church of Jesus Christ operates the Family History Library in Salt Lake City, Utah, (www.familysearch.org), the largest genealogical library in the world. Through their free online database, you can search selected census records, the International Genealogical Index, a Vital Records Index, and much more, often just with your ancestor's last name as a starting point. For more on the FHL, see IDEA 24, *The Family History Library.*

Q   What do registers contain besides the details of baptisms, marriages, or burials?

How did it go?

A   *It really depends on who was responsible for maintaining the registers as to what was recorded and thus what you will discover. They may also contain names of churchwardens and other parish officers, lists of those taking communion, and even detailed lists of parishioners. It is also common to find information of local interest—for example, descriptions of floods or heavy snow and subsequent damage to the church.*

23

Where there's a will

Wills have a singular importance, not least because of the details they frequently contain about family, relationships, property, and place of burial.

Those you think should have left wills often didn't; those that you think wouldn't often did. Expect to be both disappointed and pleasantly surprised.

Wills are one of only a handful of documents of a personal nature, apart from diaries, that might give some insight into the innermost feelings of an ancestor:

"My wife, Anne Porter, who lives separate and apart from me shall take no benefit nor be entitled nor be interested in any manner under this my will to any part of my estate." (1840)

Here's an idea for you...

In England, the superior court that was responsible for probate until 1858 was the Prerogative Court of Canterbury (PCC). The original records are now held by the British National Archives. All of these have been indexed and you can search them online at the British National Archives' website. You can also download digitized copies of the wills for a fee. Many famous wills are included, such as those of Horatio Nelson, William Shakespeare, and Jane Austen. So, choose one of your heroes or heroines and for a small fee see what they had to say in their will.

There are no rules as to who might and might not have made a will. Class and fortune (or lack of it) made no difference, and the wills of the well-to-do lie next to those of the ne'er-do-well.

Though some are dated years before, many, if not most, wills are dated shortly before the death of the testator (the deceased). There are some possible reasons for this. In the old days, you knew if you caught something nasty you were probably on your way out. Possibly, too, the expense prevented people from making their will until the last moment. The thought that writing a will might have been "tempting fate" is yet another possible reason.

If your ancestor was one of the prepared ones who left a will behind, there will be records of the legal proceedings that followed his death. The executor—the person appointed by your ancestor to handle his final affairs—would have begun the probate process, which determined the legality of the will, by scheduling a hearing with the court. The court would have heard testimony from witnesses to the will's signing and given the floor to anyone who contested it. If the court gave the will its approval, it would have been transcribed into the court record books and indexed. Probate was usually completed within a few weeks of the person's death, though there are plenty of exceptions. Very generally, though, the whole matter, from the actual making of the will to probate, took just a matter of weeks.

Take look at IDEA 18, *Become a where wolf*, for more information on how to track down a particular document.

Try another idea...

Once the court approved the probate, the deceased's estate was settled. The term "estate" generally referred to the deceased's real and personal property. Real property included land and real estate; personal property included money, jewelry, animals, and other personal items. The court typically appointed appraisers to assign value to the deceased's estate, a process that varied in length depending on the extent of the estate. Assets were then distributed to heirs or beneficiaries as directed in the will, or, in cases where no will exists, at the discretion of the court.

The original will and any ancillary documents were kept by the court. These "probate packets" can sometimes still be found in the courthouses where they were originally filed. Many probate packets and wills have also been microfilmed by the Family History Library. The packets may contain inventories and appraisal records of your ancestor's estate, notes on the testimony proceedings, records of your ancestor's financial accounts, or even receipts from the beneficiaries or heirs named in the will.

"The man that leaves no will after his death had little will before his death."
AUSTIN O'MALLEY (1858–1932), oculist and writer

Defining idea...

"You give but little when you give of your possessions. It is when you give of yourself that you truly give."

KAHLIL GIBRAN (1883–1931), Lebanese poet, artist, and philosopher

Wills may be one of the few sources that do give us a deep insight into the private lives of our ancestors. For instance, in his will, dated 1790, Charles Smith wrote:

"Item I give devise and bequeath unto my respectful friend Elizabeth Morgan all my household furniture, stock in trade, ready cash, book debts, notes of hand, and all other my estate, and effects of what nature or kind the same may be, to and for her own sole use and benefit. Item I give and bequeath unto Frances Smith, my wife, the sum of one shilling of lawful money ..."

Q   **How can I easily discover where earlier wills are kept?**

How did
it go?

A   *Figuring out where to start looking for wills and other associated documents is a two-stage process. First you have to determine in which court,
or courts, the grant may have been made, and then ascertain where the
records of that court are now kept. Do check with the record office to make
certain before visiting.*

24

The Family History Library

Truly a treasure trove of genealogical records, the FHL will surely be one of your most valuable resources.

The Family History Library was founded in 1894 by the members of the Church of Jesus Christ of Latter-day Saints in an effort to help them discover and preserve their ancestral history.

Today, it is the largest genealogical library in the world, housing a staggering number of records and resources. The FHL, based in Salt Lake City, Utah, is free and open to the public. If you can't make it to Utah, the FHL also operates more than four thousand satellite branches, called Family History Centers, around the world. (To find the center nearest you, visit www.familysearch.org/eng/library/FHC/ frameset_fhc.asp?PAGE=library_fhc_find.asp.) Materials are easily loaned from the main library to Family History Centers. And of course, the FHL's extensive holdings are cataloged and indexed for easy searching online at the FHL homepage, www.familysearch.org/eng/default.asp.

Here's an idea for you... **As with all sources, if an entry is found on the International Genealogical Index, it is vital to check with the original register because much additional information may be given.**

So what exactly can you find at the FHL? More like what *can't* you find.

The Family History Library Catalog: The definitive guide to the FHL's holdings. Here you'll be able to peruse and search for all the records and materials at the FHL, regardless of format (book, microfilm, electronic file, etc.). You can find it online at www.familysearch .org/eng/library/FHLC/frameset_fhlc.asp.

The International Genealogical Index: A listing of the names of hundreds of millions of deceased people from around the world, dating to as early as the sixteenth century. Birthdates and marriage details may also be included for some entries. The IGI is searchable online at www.familysearch.org/eng/search/frameset_search .asp?PAGE=igi/search_IGI.asp&clear_form=true.

US Social Security Death Index: A collection of records from the US Social Security Administration, which list the name, birth and death dates, Social Security number, and location of the number's issue for deceased individuals. The majority of the records date from 1962. It is online at www.familysearch.org/eng/search/ frameset_search.asp?PAGE=ssdi/search_ssdi.asp&clear_form=true.

Federal Census Records: Census returns from 1790 to 1920, many with indexes, are available for search on-site. The 1880 Census records are available for search online at www.familysearch.org/eng/search/frameset_search.asp?PAGE=census/search_ census.asp.

State, County, and Town Records: Though the records available from each jurisdiction vary, these collections are vast and incredibly useful. Among the most useful: vital records (or indexes) for states, counties, and towns; state census records; county court and probate records; city directories; and county cemetery records.

For information on more specialized genealogical libraries and collections, turn to IDEA 18, *Become a where wolf.*

Try another idea...

US Military Records: This huge collection includes pension and service files for participants in the Revolutionary War, the War of 1812, and the Civil War, and draft registrations from World War I. Also of note is the US Military Index, which lists the names of the men and women who died in service to their country in the Korean and Vietnam Wars.

Passenger and Immigration Lists: A collection of names of immigrants who came to the United States through a number of major ports between 1820 and the 1940s.

The FHL and its branches are staffed by professionals and trained volunteers, all happy to help you search their ever-growing collection of materials. Their website even includes a helpful guide for amateur genealogists as they begin their research and prepare for a visit to the Library or one of its Centers. Check it out at www .familysearch.org/eng/oibrary/FHL/frameset_library.asp?PAGE=library_preparing .asp.

How did it go?

Q **I really want to use the Family History Library to best effect. How can I learn more about the records available?**

A *The FHL regularly offers classes and lecture series that are open to the public. Lectures focus around a topic of specific interest, such as researching ancestors from a particular country or how to begin genealogical research. Classes, offered daily, cover the use of individual resources held by the Library. To register for classes or explore upcoming lectures, visit www.familysearch.org/eng/library/education/frameset_education.asp.*

25

Uncle Sam wants you!

From colonial times to the present, the United States has depended on its military might. Chances are, one of your ancestors served in the armed forces.

Military records are an excellent way to learn more about your ancestors and their contribution to the country, and more records are becoming available every day.

Though views on war may be a topic most people avoid in polite company, military records offer fascinating details about veteran ancestors. Luckily, organizations like the Family History Library and the National Archives and Records Administration (NARA) are currently undertaking massive efforts to digitize and index military records, making them available to the public for free. If you know when your ancestor served, it's now easier than ever to find the details of his service.

The Revolutionary War: Fought from 1775 to 1783, the Revolutionary War was a fight for Colonial independence from British rule. When the war began, the

Here's an idea for you… **If you want to find out what your ancestor did in World War I, be prepared to take time and persevere. Bear in mind, too, that this is probably one area of research where printed sources and the World Wide Web equal, if not outrank, manuscript sources in their ability to provide those sought-after facts.**

Defining idea… *"War is much too important a matter to be left to the generals."*
GEORGES CLEMENCEAU (1841–1929), French diplomat, poet, and dramatist

Colonies had no official military, but rather local militias. With the installation of George Washington as commander-in-chief came a centralization of military force, resulting in the Continental Army. Militia records are usually held in local archives. Pension files and Bounty-Land Warrant Applications have just begun to be digitized, and a small number are available through the NARA. For information on retrieving these files, visit the NARA website at www.archives.gov/research/arc/topics/revolutionary-war.html.

The War of 1812: From 1812 to 1815, the United States was yet again at war with Britain (and Ireland and Canada), this time over land and trade disputes. Some Americans saw it as a "second war for independence," and many joined the cause. The NARA provides access to Pension and Bounty-Land Warrant Applications, service records, discharge certificates, payrolls, and muster rolls. A complete discussion of these records can be found on the NARA website at www.archives.gov/research/military/war-of-1812.html.

The Civil War: In 1861, America went to war with itself when eleven Southern states seceded from the Union. The Confederate States of America, as they were known, claimed states rights allowed them the freedom to secede; President Abraham Lincoln and the Union states refused the right. Active warfare broke out when Confederate forces attacked Fort Sumter in 1861, and lasted until Confederate General Robert E. Lee's surrender in 1865. The NARA holds extensive records on the conflict, including service records, pension records, maps, photographs, and much more for both Union and Confederate soldiers. For information on the ever-expanding collections, visit the Civil War page on the NARA website at www.archives.gov/research/civil-war/index.html.

World War I: The first truly global war, World War I was fought from 1914 to 1918 between the Allied Powers (the United States, the United Kingdom, France, Italy, and Russia) and the Central Powers (Germany, Austria-Hungary, and the Ottoman Empire). The United States entered the conflict in 1917, spurred by the sinking of American ships and the discovery of a German proposition for Mexico to attack the United States. Thousands of soldiers were sent to fight in Europe, and many of their personnel and medical records are now held by the National Personnel

How World War I affected local communities was well covered by newspapers of the time, and the deaths of local "boys" were also frequently included. See IDEA 9, *All the news that's fit to print.*

Try another idea...

"The first casualty when war comes is truth."
HIRAM JOHNSON (1866–1945), US Senator

Defining idea...

Records Center (NPRC) in St. Louis (www.archives.gov/st-louis/military-personnel/index.html). These records are available upon request. The NARA also has Draft Registration Cards (www.archives.gov/genealogy/military/ww1/draft-registration/index.html) and burial indexes for WWI servicemen.

World War II: The second global conflict, pitting the Allied Powers (the United States, the United Kingdom, France, the Soviet Union) against the Axis Powers (Germany, Italy, Japan), was fought from 1939 to 1945. The United States entered the war against the Axis Powers in 1941 after the Japanese bombing of Pearl Harbor. Again, thousands of soldiers were sent to Europe to fight for the Allied cause. Their personnel and medical records are at the NPRC, while the NARA holds wide-ranging materials like photographs, burial records, casualty lists, prisoner of war cards, and materials on the war effort "on the homefront." A complete listing can be found on the NARA site at www.archives.gov/research/ww2/index.html.

The Korean War: The United States entered into Korea's civil war in 1950 when the Soviet Union's support of North Korea became a concern. The United States' involvement in the "police action" (war was never officially declared by the United States) lasted until the cease-fire in 1953. Personnel and medical records can be found at the NPRC. NARA offers access to burial records, casualty lists, and prisoner of war records and much more at www.archives.gov/research/korean-war/index.html.

Q   **I can't travel to the National Archives in Washington or the NPRC in St. Louis. Where else can I find military records?**

A   *The Family History Library has a number of military resources, including service records, pension records, cemetery records, and much more. A complete listing of the FHL's holdings can be found at www.familysearch .org/eng/search/RG/guide/military1.asp. Other genealogy sites, like Ancestry.com, have also begun to offer some military records online. And don't forget to check your local archives, museums, and libraries for materials pertaining to the region.*

26

For king and country

**If not "tinker or tailor" then possibly "soldier or sailor."
In yesteryear, almost every British family has been
represented in its country's armed forces. Hence, a good
place to look for ancestors.**

Over the centuries millions of Britons have
joined the Army or Navy, or more recently the
Air Force, either as volunteers at times of their
country's need or as career soldiers and sailors.

Before 1642, there was no regular standing army and the British Army per se can
be said to date from the Restoration in 1660. Conscription was unnecessary until
1916, before which the British Army was made up entirely of volunteers. Part of the
reason why this was so was that the need for men had historically been reasonably
low. Even at the height of Britain's imperial power, in the late nineteenth century,
the numbers were surprisingly low: In 1899 there were only 180,000 serving officers
and men.

Knowing where a regiment, or one of its battalions, was stationed at any particular date can be important. If it is known that a child was born in Gibraltar in 1872,
then by discovering what regiments were there at that date, information on the

Here's an idea for you... **Once you have determined the regiment—or sometimes regiments—a British ancestor served in, then see if any regimental histories have been published. The regimental museum will hold copies, as may the British National Archives' Library. Both the National Army Museum and Imperial War Museum's libraries have important collections, as does the British Library.**

father might be found using surviving army records. There are monthly returns that give the whereabouts of each regiment among the public records and a consolidated listing has been published.

The Imperial War Museum in England covers conflict from 1914 onward. The National Army Museum is responsible for the earlier period, with material dating from 1485. The lives of ordinary soldiers are well illustrated, with letters, diaries, memoirs, and poems written by men stationed in every corner of the globe. These are supplemented by letter books, war diaries, and order books, together with maps, records relating to several regiments, and more than one million photographs.

But it is at the National Archives both in the United States and the United Kingdom that the majority of records relating to those who served in the military are to be found, both for officers and enlisted men. For the British, these are almost exclusively for those discharged to pension and not for those who died in action, deserted enlisted men, or bought their way out. The records that do survive, from 1760, can be incredibly rewarding, often including considerable personal information as well as career details.

Defining idea... *"It is upon the navy, under the Providence of God, that the safety, honor, and welfare of this realm do chiefly attend."*
CHARLES II (1630–1685)

120

For those who served in the British Royal Navy, the records are again at the British National Archives (TNA). For officers these are reasonably comprehensive from the Restoration. However, the situation for ratings is very different, as it was not until 1853 that any service records were kept by the Navy. Before that date, ordinary seamen did not join the "Navy" but only individual ships for the lengths of their commissions—a few weeks or months, rarely longer than a year. It is difficult, usually impossible, to construct any service career for them and the ship's musters are one of the few places where information on ordinary seamen is to be found—though, to use these, the name of the ship needs to be known.

If not fighting "for king and country," there are other things your ancestors might have been doing. See IDEA 28, *Trades and occupations*, and IDEA 29, *Professions and professionals*.

Try another idea...

The constant threat of invasion and civil unrest meant that many men were members of the county militia regiments, yeomanries, or sea fencibles. For the earlier years, the majority of the records relating to these men are to be found in county record offices; later records may also be held locally or are to be found at the British National Archives (TNA). The US National Archives and Record Administration (NARA) does not include information on militias, because these are generally held locally.

The chances of anyone not having an ancestor who served in one of the armed forces is slim and the information that may be discovered, with a little perseverance, is considerable. And it may have been a "family thing" with several generations serving in the Army, Navy, or perhaps the Royal Marines, whose records, too, are to be found at TNA.

How did
it go?

**Q   I have been told that I have an ancestor who served at Waterloo.
How can I find out if this is true?**

A   *If all those who were said to have served at Waterloo were added up, the
number would be many, many times the actual number who were really
there. There are no special or separate service records for those who
fought at the great battles and for those discharged to pension; they will
be among other service records. For all those discharged before 1855, the
extant records have been indexed into TNA's online catalog. So if you know
this particular ancestor's name you can search this source. The first true
British military campaign medal was awarded to all those who took part in
the battles of Waterloo, Ligny, and Quatre Bras, 16–18 June 1815, regardless of rank. Again, the records are at TNA.*

**Q   I just got a regimental history book for the cavalry brigade my
father's Uncle Henry served in. Will I be able to find out much
about him from there?**

A   *Sadly, no. It's unlikely that your ancestor will be mentioned by name.
However, a great deal of information will be given about the history of the
regiment—where it went in the world and what battles and major national
and international events it was involved in—and that could lead you in
some more fruitful directions.*

27

Apprenticeship and apprentices

Apprenticeship indentures can be an invaluable source for discovering the origins of a tradesman or artisan among your ancestors.

Apprenticeship, as a means of training for work, has existed since time immemorial. Nearly every trade required proper training for those who worked within it.

Before high school and college were the norm, your ancestor may have been an apprentice. Young men were often apprenticed to local craftsmen and professionals to learn the skills needed to pursue a career. Though rarer, young women were sometimes also apprenticed, learning "ladylike" trades, such as millinery and baking. If you know that your ancestor practiced a trade or craft, uncovering the details of his training may help you create a better picture of him and his life.

An apprentice would be bound to his master or mistress for a fixed period to learn his trade or craft, during which time he would usually be housed, fed, and clothed at his master's expense. The rules relating to age and the term of the apprenticeship varied a little over time, but essentially apprenticeship was for a seven-year period, ending between the ages of 19 and 21. A general rule of thumb, therefore, is that most apprenticeships began when the child was 12 to 15, although there are exceptions. The apprentice undertook to obey certain rules relating to his conduct and was generally forbidden to marry until his apprenticeship was completed. All these conditions were laid out in a formal agreement called the apprenticeship indenture.

For those parents who could afford it, a trade and master were chosen, an indenture was prepared, and a sum or premium was handed over. The fee charged for the apprenticeship varied according to how prestigious the career was and how much money the apprentice could expect to make when finished with his training. The child would then spend the next seven years learning and using the tools of his trade, ultimately producing a "master piece" that embodied all he had learned. Once his apprenticeship was over, the young man was free to open his own business and take his own apprentices.

"There is no worse apprentice than the one who doesn't want to know."

SPANISH PROVERB

The Dickensian view that all apprentices were ill-treated, starved, and beaten is probably far from the truth. The purpose of apprenticeship was to produce the next generation of tradesmen and craftsmen of the highest standard. Then, just as now, it was realized that only by careful nurturing and good treatment (by their standards) would this be achieved. Many apprentices stayed on where they had been apprenticed, eventually marrying and raising families of their own.

Indentures can be an invaluable source for discovering where an ancestor came from or where he went. Since most date to the colonial era, indenture documents can be hard to find, though records of apprenticeships may exist on the county level or in your family's historical papers. You might also be able to puzzle out the details of your ancestor's apprenticeship by checking census returns for what would be his early teenage years. Was he living at home, or at another address? Could it be his master's home? Alternatively, perhaps your ancestor's parents formally appointed his master as his guardian. Records for those proceedings would be found in the county court and primarily cover colonial times.

More information about researching African-American history can be found at IDEA 30, *African-American research*.

Try another idea...

"The profession of a prostitute is the only career in which the maximum income is paid to the newest apprentice."
WILLIAM BOOTH (1829–1912)

Defining idea...

125

How did it go?

Q **An ancestor of mine is listed in the 1880 census as a boot- and shoemaker. He was born around 1855 and I would like to find out where he was apprenticed, and to whom. What are my chances?**

A *Try to find if his father or an uncle were also in the same trade, or even a much older brother. If that is the case then probably he was trained by one of them, without any formal apprenticeship. See if you can find him in the 1870 census because he may have been living in his master's home at the time.*

Q **Would the boys and girls have been apprenticed locally or might they have gone away somewhere?**

A *Sometimes, in the case of very poor families, neither the children nor their parents had any real say in where the children were to be sent. Often, however, the apprenticeships were local.*

28
Trades and occupations

Were your ancestors peddlers or paupers; laborers or lacemakers; clockmakers or chefs; or even working in the "oldest profession"? Find out.

Cooper: A barrel maker

Cordwainer: A shoemaker

Milliner: A person who makes or sells women's hats

Sawyer: A person who cuts logs or lumber

Wheelwright: A person who made carriage wheels

The names and meanings of obsolete occupations such as these have been lost in the mists of time as industrialization and mechanization brought massive changes to society. They have been replaced by occupations such as field sales manager, IT consultant, executive, employee relations officer, and animal psychologist.

Some family historians spend a tremendous amount of time and effort locating their ancestors' birth, death, and marriage details but pay little attention to what their ancestors actually did for a living. Just as we do today, our ancestors spent most of

Here's an idea for you... **Virtually every trade required proper training for those who worked within it, so look for the apprenticeship records for your forebears. Many archives contain details about the wheres, whens, and hows for colonial apprentices. Armed with the occupation of your ancestors, you could find fascinating new paths for your research.**

their waking hours working—be they rat catchers, watchmakers, or bricklayers, they had to have a job to survive.

You might like to consider spending some time creating a through-life record for your ancestors, creating "a picture" of their lives. You might want to discover why someone did a specific job, whether they had more than one job or if historical events affected their occupational choices. Along the way, you could also discover if their workplaces still exist or if they worked from home.

So, what were your ancestors' occupations? Bear in mind that it was often your ancestors themselves giving this information and, of course, it's all a matter of interpretation. Thus, an ancestor may describe himself simultaneously as a chimney sweep or laborer, or socially upgrade himself to become an artisan. It is not uncommon for some official records to require only the occupation of the head of the household, or the male, thus allowing a married woman's occupation to be invisible.

To determine someone's occupation, try locating the record of their marriage or death, or the birth or marriage of their children. Once you have ascertained an occupation, you can look at other records that can help you add to the information you already have.

Census records from 1850 onward list the occupations of every adult over age fifteen in a household. You can check successive censuses (recorded every ten years) to see how occupations changed. Trade and city directories were compiled annually, and for large towns these have often survived from about the mid-nineteenth century. These are also extremely useful, often listing the occupation in addition to the home address, allowing you to track people between the census years. Again, checking successive editions can show changes in an occupation. Copies of directories can be found in local libraries and the FHL. Newspapers are another useful source—articles naming people usually give their occupation. Wills, probate records, and military records can also provide valuable information.

To discover if your ancestor had any formal education, look at IDEA 12, *Reading, 'riting, 'rithmetic.*

Try another idea...

A number of occupations were regulated by legislation. Some required a license, sometimes to ensure adequate competence or to ensure that the law was obeyed. These records can often be found at local county courthouses.

Surviving employment records should be found at the relevant local archives where the business was based. There are a number of dedicated archives covering specific occupations while others hold specialist collections, such as those relating to trade union records.

Once you have a full career record for any ancestors, you can begin to intertwine it with their day-to-day life events and the wider history unfolding around them. This will help you to determine why they had that occupation and what made them the way they were. It really can bring the individuals to life.

"We have not all had the good fortune to be ladies. We have not all been generals, or poets, or statesmen; but when the toast works down to the babies, we stand on common ground."
MARK TWAIN (1835–1910)

Defining idea...

How did it go?

Q   How do I find the meaning of a specific occupation?

A   *The meanings of the more commonly known occupations can be found in an ordinary dictionary. For information on more obsolete terms, consult one of the original dictionaries dating from the eighteenth or nineteenth centuries—they can be found in your local archive or at the library. It is also worth searching the Internet because there is quite a lot to be found online and there are also some occupation-related mailing lists that you can sub-scribe to. In addition, numerous specialist publications have been produced that list unusual occupations and are aimed at local and family historians. Some of them include facsimiles of old books. There are also a number of books about researching specific occupations, be it midwives or publicans. Many of these are available to purchase or can be found through your local library. A to Zax by Barbara J. Evens is a great source to consult.*

Q   So why might someone have had more than one job or trade?

A   *Apart from soldiers or sailors, who would also have had a civilian trade, many other people had trades that complemented each other, such as printer and publisher, auctioneer and valuer, carpenter and joiner—many of which have survived to the present day. A lot of other dual occupations were seasonal, such as farm laborer during the summer months and brew-ery worker in the winter. These seasonal occupations may be missed from a census return but can be discovered through the sources already discussed or by delving into the local history of an area.*

29

Professions and professionals

Architects, doctors, trade workers, lawyers, dentists, and their ilk: professionals who belonged to a professional organization or union can be easier to trace.

The majority of professions have been regulated by organizations, which have granted qualifications, governed the professionals in their good practice, and kept those all-important records.

It is worth contacting the governing body of any profession to see what records exist and which of them might include information on your forebears. A search of the Internet will almost certainly take you to the website of the organization, which itself may cover the information you want, as well as how to access the material.

It is often very useful to know what was entailed in any profession—or trade or other occupation for that matter—and there are very many books available. These range from relatively cheap books to weighty tomes produced by academics. Usually the former are sufficient to give a good background and often include illustrations that enhance the text and bring the past to life. Understanding the past often comes from an appreciation of what our ancestors actually did, day to day; what it entailed and what this meant for their own lives and those of their families. Many professionals and others kept diaries of their lives and what their work involved. See if you can find anything for the relevant time and occupation of your ancestors.

These governing bodies frequently published registers or yearbooks giving the names and qualifications of their members, plus the addresses at which they practiced. For doctors, there is the Directory of Physicians in the United States, or the American Medical Association's Deceased Physician File, which covers 1864 to 1970 (and is available on microfilm at the Family History Library). For lawyers there is the American Bar Association Member Directory. There are many, many others—for nurses, architects, teachers, and so forth. Similarly, over the years, many cumulative lists of professionals have been produced, under their chosen career, by interested individuals or a related organization. These are going to be found in specialist libraries or archives; some may be available online.

These days, all professionals are required to have some kind of formal training; in most cases, this means attending college. All colleges and universities have lists of alumni, often dedicating a whole staff to keeping tabs on the achievements of its former students. If you know where your ancestor studied, check with the alumni office of the school to see what they might have on file about him. Often, these searches will turn up addresses, marriage announcements, or details about places of employment.

Not a doctor or a lawyer, but a peddler or farm worker? Then try IDEA 28, *Trades and occupations.*

Try another idea...

If your ancestor's collar was more blue than white, chances are good he belonged to a trade union. A great place to start looking is the American Federation of Labor and the Congress of Industrial Organizations, better known as the AFL-CIO. The AFL-CIO represents 54 national and international labor unions, among them unions for electrical workers, bakers, writers, actors, teachers, longshoremen, and many, many others. The AFL-CIO's website lists links to the websites of individual organizations (www.aflcio.org/aboutus/unions/), all of which offer contact information for learning more about the unions and their members.

Those from the professions are more likely to have left wills than others and this can be a useful source for family details, possibly used in conjunction with census returns. And they are also likely to appear in the trade directories from the early and mid-nineteenth century. In fact, the earliest directories were lists of professionals, such as surgeons and lawyers, together with the major tradesmen.

Professional ancestors may be easier to trace because of the many specialist sources available, but a profession was, and is, simply another occupation and professionals were treated no different when it came to registering the births of their children or being recorded in the census.

"A professional is a man who can do his best at a time when he doesn't particularly feel like it."
ALISTAIR COOKE (1908–2005), broadcast journalist

Defining idea...

How did it go?

Q **The family I am researching all seem to have been laborers and the like. Suddenly I have found one in a census described as a "lawyer." Can this be right? How can I find out more?**

A *This is probably one of the most common errors to be made when reading some census entries, and even birth, marriage, and death certificates. Your ancestor was probably a "sawyer" not a "lawyer." The two letters, L and S, are frequently indistinguishable; so have another closer look at the entry. Another thing to watch out for is exaggeration. Many an agricultural laborer appears as a farmer at his death. Even the most humble get themselves entered as "gentleman" occasionally. Soldiers become officers and dishwashers become restauranteurs.*

Q **My dad says my mom's mom was in the "oldest profession." What is that?**

A *Ask your mother. On second thought, no, best not! There are some parts of your family history you may need to tiptoe carefully around.*

30
African-American research

The practice of slavery has blurred the histories of many African-Americans. Reclaim your family's story through your research.

Tracing your early African-American roots can be tricky, but close reading and specialized sources can help you uncover the past.

Slavery was introduced to the American colonies in the 1620s by Dutch traders and lasted more than 200 years before being abolished by the Emancipation Proclamation of 1862 and the Thirteenth Amendment to the Constitution (1865). Sadly, in the intervening years, slaves were treated as property, not people, and researching their history can be difficult. But much can be revealed about the rich past of African-Americans if you look in the right places.

CENSUS SCHEDULES

If you know the name of the slave owner, look for him on federal census returns. From 1790 to 1850, returns will show the number of slaves who lived in a given home. The 1850 and 1860 census schedules list the sex and age of slaves held by

Here's an idea for you... **Check if there is a local history society or someone undertaking a one-place study covering your area of interest, and tap into this fantastic source of "local" knowledge.**

the head of the house. The federal census mortality schedules from those years will also give the names of slaves who died. From 1870 on, all African-American people are listed in the census. You can access indexes for these records through the Family History Library (www.familysearch.org/eng/default.asp) or the National Archives and Records Administration (www.archives.gov/genealogy/census/).

FREEDMAN'S SAVINGS AND TRUST RECORDS

Established in 1865 as a bank for freed slaves, the Freedman's Savings and Trust's records contain some of the most extensive details on former slaves. Files include information including name, age, physical appearance, family members, residence, occupation, and even the name of the former slave owner, in some early records. The NARA has these files on microfilm, though they are not indexed. The deposit ledgers for accounts, however, are indexed. You can learn more at www.archives .gov/publications/ref-info-papers/108/index.html#savings.

BUREAU OF REFUGEES, FREEDMEN, AND ABANDONED LANDS

The Bureau of Refugees, Freedmen, and Abandoned Lands was created in 1865 to handle post–Civil War issues pertaining to freed slaves and abandoned land. An essential function of the bureau was aiding freedmen, providing food and clothing, helping to reunite families, assisting with legal disputes, etc. The Bureau's records are wide-ranging, including everything from physical descriptions to military documentation. A listing of the exhaustive files can be found at www.archives.gov/ publications/ref-info-papers/108/index.html#access.

Finding your ancestors in these specialized sources can give you leads to follow in other, more general sources. Don't neglect to look for your African-American ancestors' names in:

- Birth, death, and marriage records
- Military records
- Tax returns
- Land deeds
- City directories
- Newspapers

Both the Family History Library and the National Archives and Records Administration offer tutorials on starting your genealogical research. You can find the FHL guide at www .familysearch.org/eng/docs/36928_ african_american_quick_guide.pdf and a more in-depth discussion of the records that will be of the most help to you at www .familysearch.org/eng/docs/36367_african_ american_records.pdf. Both of these guides have useful bibliographies. The NARA guides to African-American records is available at www.archives.gov/genealogy/heritage/ african-american/and www.archives.gov/ publications/ref-info-papers/108/index.html.

Try another idea...

As you gather more information about your family it is very important to organize your research properly, following the golden rules of clarity, convenience, and completeness. For more tips on achieving this, see IDEA 19, *Files, formats, and family trees.*

Defining idea...

"It matters not how a man dies, but how he lives. The act of dying is not of importance, it lasts so short a time."
SAMUEL JOHNSON (1709–1784), lexicographer, critic, and poet

How did it go?

Q **I'm having a hard time finding my ancestors in all of these records, and I'd like to hire a professional who specializes in African-American genealogy.**

A *The Afro-American Historical and Genealogical Society (AAHGS) is a research service dedicated to providing genealogical resources to people of African descent. While the members of the AAHGS do not perform genea-logical research for individuals, they can direct you to local chapters, whose members can help, or refer you to specialized genealogists. To learn more about the AAHGS and its services, visit www.aahgs.org/.*

31

Arms and the man

Heraldry is all around us—on inn signs, in stained-glass church windows, and as hatchments (armorial bearings of the dead)—and perhaps on the spoons in your cutlery drawer.

Personal and civic heraldry have been with us for the greater part of the last millennium. If your ancestors were from Europe, get your crayons out—it's coloring time.

Imagine a football match with all the players wearing the same colored jersey. Not only would the referee be confused but also the teams themselves wouldn't know which players were theirs and which weren't. It was the same in medieval times when it was necessary in battle to be able to distinguish between friend and foe. Before the introduction of distinctive colors and badges for the opposing sides, there was frequently great confusion and many a disaster.

Initially, brightly colored banners were used for identification, often with some form of emblem. This idea extended itself to shields and then to surcoats worn over chain mail (hence the term coat of arms). With the advent of tournaments as popular forms of entertainment, armor became much more elaborate and the emblem or "device" was extended to the liveries worn by servants and members of the household.

The simplest arms are usually the oldest, and those with no crest or motto probably date from before the fifteenth century. More recent grants of arms tend to feature elements that associate the bearer with his or her career. For instance, Lord Zuckerman's arms pay tribute to his work for London Zoo and so feature a gorilla; Elton John's arms incorporate a keyboard.

"Reading" a coat of arms may look totally impossible, but you can easily break it down into a number of parts, each with its own purpose and meaning. There are plenty of books around that go into the fine detail. A "complete achievement" consists of a shield of arms, usually with the addition of a crest born on a helmet, and frequently with a motto below. The crest was originally there to ward off blows to the head and often took the form of a device fashioned out of boiled leather. Fabulous birds, beasts, and inanimate objects, such as ships and castles, were all popular.

Here's an idea for you... **Turn your next pub crawl into an heraldic adventure by only visiting those hostelries named after coats of arms or badges or other elements taken from the world of heraldry. Then see if you can find out why the pub is called what it is.**

Attached to the helmet is the mantling, which resembles and derives from the material used to protect the helmet and the head from the extreme heat of the sun encountered during the Crusades. Supporters, usually found in pairs on either side of the shield, are restricted to the more illustrious achievements and to civic arms.

The shield itself is where the "shorthand for history" is to be found. As armigerous families intermarried, so the shields became divided and quartered (any number of even parts, not just four) according to strict rules. And so the simplest of arms could evolve, becoming more and more complicated over time, but encompassing the history of the family.

The motto has far more obscure origins. In some cases it may have derived from an ancient battle cry but it may relate to a more important happening in the history of the family, a religious bias, or even simply a pun on the name. The Barnard family, whose arms depict a black bear with a gold muzzle, uses the motto "Bear and Forbear."

Civic heraldry, which is connected with towns and cities, usually tells something of their history or connection with a particular family. For example, in the arms of Birmingham, two of the most prominent families are represented: the de Bermingham family by gold lozenges; and the Calthorpe family by an ermine fess (bar).

The heraldry all around us is far more than just decoration. Once interpreted, the origin and meaning of any particular coat of arms can expand the knowledge and understanding of both family and local history.

"The boast of heraldry, the pomp of power,
And all that beauty, all that wealth e'er gave,
Awaits alike th' inevitable hour.
The paths of glory lead but to the grave."
THOMAS GRAY (1716–1771), "Elegy Written in a Country Churchyard"

Defining idea...

How did
it go?

Q   **My name is Hewitt, which I have discovered is the family name of the Earls of Lifford. I have also found out that there are several Hewitt arms, all slightly different. Which one can I use?**

A   *Probably none of them. If your family was ever entitled to a coat of arms then it is very unlikely that this is something that would be forgotten by the generations. It is enormously important to remember that arms belong to a family and not to a name.*

Q   **I've seen people selling coats of arms and name origins. Are they likely to have the correct one for me?**

A   *There are lots of companies that will sell you computer printouts of coats of arms just based on your surname. They can look great on the wall but don't rush off and have your stationery reprinted or get a seal made until you have proved these belong to your family as well.*

32

Manors maketh man

In England, lords and laborers all contributed to the extraordinary records of the manorial courts, which can reveal the history of your English ancestors from the twelfth century.

No coat of arms in your family? Manorial documents are among the few types of records where genealogical information about ordinary people—rather than the upper classes—is likely to survive from medieval times.

The manor was at the center of feudal society and was essentially the government of the local community in medieval times. It not only had administrative control but also functioned as a court of law for minor, and some not so minor, offenses. The owner of the manor, the lord, was answerable to the king. Everyone had their roles within a strict order and it was extremely difficult to rise above those positions.

Within the manor, land could be held in several ways. The first was by "customary tenure"—that is, by tradition in return for working on the lord's own land. The descent of these holdings was governed by "custom," or accepted rules of the manor in question. The most common form of customary tenure was known as "copyhold

The difficulties of using manorial documents include the handwriting and language, which in medieval times was Latin. English became more common in Tudor times, but many manorial court records continued in Latin until the eighteenth century. To unravel these records, check out two online tutorials— one on paleography (old handwriting) and one on Latin—produced by the British National Archives. These are really user-friendly and are an excellent idea even for the absolute novice.

tenure," because each tenant was given a copy of the entry in the manor court roll that recorded his succession.

Freehold land was usually held in return for a fixed rent. Its descent was not governed by the manor but freeholders were still subject to manorial jurisdiction in other respects, so that they do also appear in the records. Others held leasehold land. Over the centuries the authority of the lord of the manor was reduced, although the last vestiges of the copyhold system survived until 1922.

The records of the lords of the manor and the manorial courts still exist and in some places go back centuries, from the present day back to well before the commencement of parish records. The area governed by a manor court was usually quite different from the parish's area: Any one manor may have within its boundary the whole or parts of one or more parishes, and vice versa.

There were two main types of manorial court, both of which produced comprehensive records of their meetings. The court leet dealt with minor offenses, such as straying cattle, ditches not being cleared, hedges not being maintained, or selling underweight goods (and even with more serious offenses in earlier times).

Defining idea...

"If a man owns land, the land owns him."
RALPH WALDO EMERSON
(1803–1882), essayist, poet, and philosopher

The most useful manorial records are those generated by the Court Baron, which met several times each year. This business would include the reporting of tenants' deaths—in theory, freehold as well as customary tenants —and the payment to the lord of the corresponding feudal due, a fine or heriot. When the heir of a dead customary tenant succeeded, the "surrender" of the land and the "admission" of the new tenant would be recorded, the relationship between the two usually being noted. Occasionally, there are payments noted for the marriages of the daughters of customary tenants or records of the remarriage of widows. Other tenants will be named in the records: As officials or jurors, they may be noted as absent, or they may be fined, "amerced," for some minor offense.

Another important record is the Manorial Survey. Over time, these assumed different forms: Usually they include at least a list of the names of the manorial tenants, and may give much fuller information. The "custumal," common in the twelfth and thirteenth centuries, recorded the tenants, their holdings, and their obligations to the lord; the "extent," a valuation of the manor; and the "rental," which listed tenants and the rents payable. Occasionally a plan of the manorial extents exists that is associated with the rental.

Most manorial records are private, not public, and so their survival has been more a matter of luck than of routine. Large numbers of medieval documents have been lost. For known surviving records, and their location, there is an official listing—the Manorial Documents Register—held at the British National

Manorial records are ideally used together with contemporary maps and plans. See IDEA 17, *How does the land lie?*

Try another idea...

"You had better have a rich landlord ... you will find that every man is worse for being poor."
GEORGE BERNARD SHAW
(1856–1950)

Defining idea...

Archives (TNA). For a few counties only, the listing is available online. Most court records will be found in the county record office, but many are still in private hands or even overseas. TNA has a large collection of records for Crown manors.

Manor court records can reveal much about our ancestors' lives. Looking through these documents, it is possible to trace the changes in land holdings, which can be the only record in earlier times of deaths, marriage, and inheritance.

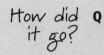

Q   I have managed to locate where some manorial records are held. Is there anything useful I can read before going to see them?

A   *A volume in the Victoria County History series might help. This could tell you which families were lords of the manor and give you other useful information. Your local reference library may have a complete set of the VCH.*

Q   Some of the records I have found seem to be held in a record office for a completely different county. Why might this be?

A   *Many lords, particularly in more recent centuries, had their "seat" far away from the manors they owned; hence, the documentation can be far removed from the place it refers to. This is why the Manorial Documents Register is so important.*

33

Crime and punishment

For the family historian, crime really does pay. Criminal ancestors left an extensive paper trail, allowing you to uncover a tremendous amount of information about them.

Your ancestors would, of course, never have been involved in anything really nasty—or would they?

There is an extremely good chance that one of your ancestors has appeared in the criminal courts either as a defendant, plaintiff, victim, witness, or even as a member of the jury, so legal records are well worth looking into.

Keep a close eye out for any mention of your ancestor, his family, or his business associates in historical local newspapers, especially those from small towns. Just as today, local papers covered smaller stories that wouldn't have gained national attention, and your ancestor's court case could have been one of them. Check to see if the newspapers you're searching have police blotters, which run down arrests made by local law enforcement. Use the arrest date as a starting point for searching court files.

Reasons for crime were as hotly discussed in the past as they are today. Once you have located the details of a specific court case, trawl through the local newspapers to see if they contain any additional information such as eyewitness reports of the offense.

If your ancestor was unfortunate enough to be embraced by the long arm of the law, jail or prison records will document his time in the penal system.

Finding a prisoner who was held at a city, county, or state jail can usually be accomplished by contacting the state department of corrections or the county courthouse. Many states have online inmate locators, which will tell you when and where an individual was held. Not all states have this feature, and very few have locators with records that go back far enough to help you in your search. In these cases, you should contact the state department directly about your inquiry. You can find a complete listing of state corrections departments at http://answers .usa.gov/cgi-bin/gsa_ict.cfg/php/enduser/std_adp.php?p_faqid=5849.

If your ancestor served time in a federal prison, he will be on record with the Federal Bureau of Prisons. While the BOP's website offers an inmate locator, the files only date back to 1982. To find a prisoner released before that year, contact the Office of Communications and Archives (www.bop.gov/inmate_locator/inmates_ b4_1982.jsp). Historic federal inmate files are also held at National Archives. Details on the NARA's holdings can be found at www.archives.gov/research/prisons.html.

For more general searches, you can also try Prison Search (www.ancestorhunt.com/ genealogical_prison_records), which delves into both court and penal records.

Family historians who take the time to research these types of legal documents will often be pleasantly surprised by the rewards that are in store. The amount of information contained within a court file can vary greatly from one case to another and from one region of the country to another. In general, you should hope to find dates and places of births, marriages, and deaths; the names and ages of children; information about your relatives' residences; and financial and employment information.

Begin your prowl and discover what's found where within the giant labyrinth of archives, libraries, and record repositories. Try IDEA 18, *Become a where wolf*.

Try another idea...

The records are not always easy to read, but sometimes the material they contain is pure gold, with the trial details providing a fascinating insight into our ancestors' lives and the world they lived in. In addition, they'll allow you to discover if you are descended from a sinner or a saint.

"If you can't get rid of the skeleton in your closet, you'd best teach it to dance."
GEORGE BERNARD SHAW
(1856–1950)

Defining idea...

How did it go?

Q   How do I find out about my police officer ancestor?

A   Records are either retained by the police themselves or deposited at the appropriate record office. Check with your state's division of criminal justice services for information about police officer registries.

Q   There is a family story that a criminal ancestor was transported to America from England. How do I find more information?

A   From the seventeenth century, royal pardons were granted to many condemned convicts, on condition that they were transported to work on plantations in the American colonies. Usually the sentences were for seven or fourteen years but many were transported for life. In all, 56,000 people were transported. Transportation ceased on the outbreak of the Revolutionary War in 1776. Lists of references to convicts transported to America have been indexed and published. Transportation resumed in 1787 with a new destination: Australia. By 1830, it was becoming very expensive and the end of transportation to New South Wales finally came after the discovery of gold and the resulting gold rush of 1851. A further 9,500 convicts were sent to Western Australia between 1850 and 1868, when the transportation system finally ended. Many of these records have been indexed.

34

Let's get out of here

Emigration has generated a wide variety of records, which, due to their very origins, need to be hunted for in a number of different places.

The grass has always been greener somewhere else. And if the somewhere else was another country or colony, then emigration resulted. Single members to extended families all sought a better life away from the mother country.

Over the centuries, people have come to America to travel, to explore, to seek fame and fortune, to trade, to colonize, and to govern. Your ancestors were among them.

Looking for an ancestor who came to America can be a difficult but ultimately very rewarding process. Because the US government did not require lists of immigrants entering the country until 1820, and because immigration was handled on the state, not federal, level until 1820, records prior to that year can sometimes be difficult to locate. And everyone has heard the way immigrants "Americanized"

Here's an idea for you...

Take a look in the local newspapers covering the areas where your ancestors lived. Obituaries of emigrant ancestors can cover in surprising detail all aspects of their lives, including the names of relatives in the old country and occasionally place of birth.

their names when they arrived on these shores; variations in spellings can also make the search more difficult. But perseverance will yield many important details about your ancestor's first days in America.

The earliest immigrants came by ship into one of America's many ports. Though New York's Ellis Island is perhaps the best-known port, millions of immigrants also came through Boston, Philadelphia, New Orleans, and San Francisco, and more than one hundred minor ports. For ancestors who arrived here after 1820, there will be written documentation of their arrival in the form of entries on passenger lists known as Customs Lists. Lists from 1820 to 1893 will list the basics, including name, age, nation of origin, and possibly occupation. After 1893, however, the lists change dramatically. From that point on, immigration law dictated that passenger lists needed to include the information above, as well as details on literacy, former residence, criminal history, medical history, final destination, and physical description.

Many passenger lists have been indexed and published, or are in the process thereof. Microfilm of lists can be found at the National Archives and the Family History Library; online databases of these materials are also springing up on the web. For a complete listing of microfilmed passenger lists held by the NARA, go to www.archives.gov/genealogy/immigration/passenger-arrival.html. Passenger lists documenting the millions of immigrants who passed through Ellis Island are available at www.ellisisland.org/search/passSearch.asp?, and are completely free to search.

If your ancestor came to this country before specific records were required, you'll have to be a bit more creative in your search. Naturalization records can help you pinpoint when your family member arrived and give you some detail about his life before arrival here. Check census returns for years that included immigration and naturalization information to help start your search. But be aware that naturalization records would have been kept on the county level before 1906, when the Immigration and Naturalization Service was introduced.

Slabs, headstones, memorials, crematoria, and churchyards can all bring the dead back to life. Look at IDEA 11, *Writ in stone.*

Try another idea...

Research studies into emigration now acknowledge the important role played by newspapers and the notices they carried, particularly in providing information about the means of emigration—information about the departure and arrival of ships and advertisements giving the names of local agents through whom passages might be arranged are all listed. These newspapers also carried details of land that was available to purchase by prospective immigrants.

A more sophisticated means of drawing attention to the mechanics of emigration were perhaps the published letters that also appeared in the newspapers—particularly from the 1800s, a period of increased emigration mainly in reaction to depressed circumstances affecting the linen industry and trade. These were letters ostensibly written by passengers who had made the crossing and whose first thought on arrival was apparently to write to the newspaper. The stories they told of relative success and, above all perhaps, satisfaction with their initial decision to make the move, must have provided the reassurance that intending emigrants wanted to hear. The NARA holds many historical foreign newspapers.

"All travel has its advantages. If the passenger visits better countries, he may learn to improve his own. And if fortune carries him to worse, he may learn to enjoy it."
SAMUEL JOHNSON (1709–1784), lexicographer, critic, and poet

Defining idea...

How did it go? **Q   Do passport records survive?**

A   *The US Department of State has issued passports since 1789, but they have only been required for overseas travel since 1941. The NARA holds records for passport applications from 1795 to 1925, and the Department of State holds the records from 1925 forward. Finding a record for your ancestor's application could be a goldmine of information: Passport applications require information on place and date of birth, physical description, naturalization, and sometimes occupation. Passport applications after 1914 may be particularly rewarding, as these applications required a photo of the individual applying. For more information about passports and a complete listing of the NARA's passport records, visit www.archives.gov/genealogy/passport/. For more information about the Department of State's holdings, visit http://travel.state.gov/passport/services/copies/copies_872.html.*

35

Aliens in the family

Your ancestors may have been among the refugees, merchants, and entrepreneurs who, over the centuries, decided that the grass was greener in Britain and made the move.

From time immemorial, individuals and families from overseas relocated to the British Isles to find work, escape from religious or political persecution, or simply seek a better life.

Some immigrants stayed in Britain for only a short time, either going back home or moving on again, while others made it their permanent home. Geography has always made England a natural destination for emigrants from the continent of Europe. Immigration during recent years tends to make people forget that the earliest immigrants came not as refugees but were usually invited to come by the Crown or government of the day. From as far back as Henry I in 1113, immigrants were offered asylum for both altruistic and selfish reasons, knowing that the country would benefit from their knowledge and skills.

After Henry VIII split from the Church of Rome, England became a place of exile for Protestants fleeing persecution in Europe. These included French Protestants

Here's an idea for you...

If you have any interest in migration to the UK, discover *Moving Here* (www.movinghere.org.uk), a website that focuses on the experiences of the Jewish (from Eastern Europe), Irish, and people from the Caribbean and South Asia from the 1840s to the present day. Also included is information on how you can use these resources for your own research. This website offers free access, for personal and educational use, to online versions of original material related to migration, including photographs, personal papers, government documents, maps, and art objects, as well as a collection of sound recordings and video clips.

Defining idea...

"Immigrant, n. An unenlightened person who thinks one country better than another."
AMBROSE BIERCE (1842–1914),
The Devil's Dictionary

from as early as the sixteenth century, and especially the Huguenots and Walloons from the late seventeenth century, plus exiles from the Palatinate in the early eighteenth century. During the eighteenth and nineteenth centuries, further Protestant refugees flooded into Britain, notably those fleeing from the French Revolution in 1789. There were no controls on immigration into England until the beginning of the war with France in 1793.

During the nineteenth century, unemployment and overpopulation in Ireland resulted in many laborers coming to England to find work, particularly between 1815 and 1830. Famine in Ireland between 1845 and 1851 caused thousands more to emigrate to England and Scotland, and, of course, to the United States.

Italians arrived from the early nineteenth century, congregating around Clerkenwell in London, and later spreading into Soho. The first settlers were craftsmen and precision instrument makers, as well as those bringing Italian ice cream to the British.

In 1290, Edward I had expelled all Jews from England, and they were not readmitted until the Commonwealth under Cromwell, in 1656. Russian and Polish Jews began to arrive in the last two decades of the nineteenth century and then again during the periods of Jewish persecution leading up to World War II.

Family photographs may include clues to origins of immigrant ancestors. For more, see IDEA 46, *Families in focus*.

Try another idea...

Following the 1948 British Nationality Act, there began the first major immigration of West Indians in large numbers to their "mother country."

At an early date, it became necessary to introduce a procedure for admitting foreigners to all or some of the privileges of a natural-born British subject. Before 1844, there were two methods of obtaining the privileges of a native: (1) by taking out an "act of naturalization," or (2) by "letters of denization." The most important difference was that in the case of denization the privileges conveyed were not retrospective but commenced only from the date of the grant—aliens were not entitled to hold land in the country, and letters of denization were not sufficient to enable a man to inherit, nor confer any benefit on children born previous to the date of the grant.

The records of denization and naturalization, which date from about 1400, are to be found mainly at the British National Archives (TNA). There are, fortunately, combined indexes to all the classes and collections of records concerned. In particular, all naturalizations from 1844 to 1936 are indexed into TNA's online catalog. Even so, the records held at TNA are sparse and difficult to use. Lists of ships' passengers entering from abroad survive in the public records from 1890 to 1960 but they are only for vessels sailing from places outside Europe. There are no comparable lists or registers concerned with people arriving in the UK by air.

"Immigration is the sincerest form of flattery."
JACK PAAR (1918–2004), talk-show host and comedian

Defining idea...

Discovering you have an immigrant family in your past should come as no surprise—most of us do. With luck and perseverance your research may take you to another country and the records held there. It is sure to raise the question: "Why did they come to the UK?"

How did it go?

Q   I have found a branch of my family in the census returns, but it just says they were "born in Prussia." Will I be able to find their whereabouts in Prussia? And where was Prussia anyway?

A   *Prussia was a north German state stretching eastward from the Low Countries out along the Baltic coast into current-day Poland. It was dissolved in 1947, following World War II. To track your relatives, try looking for specific locations in the records of naturalization at the National Archives, and keep an eye out for any possible brothers or uncles, too. Also, the Anglo-German Family History Society might be able to help you.*

Q   I have a similar problem, as the census returns only say "born in Ireland."

A   *As all of Ireland was part of Great Britain until 1922, there will be no naturalization records to help. So, make sure you check all the available census returns because one of them might include the town in Ireland where they were born. It's no consolation, but the surviving returns for Ireland similarly only state "England" for place of birth.*

36

Wading into the gene pool

Not too long ago, you were the child of your father, according to your mother. Today, genetics can help in determining our origins, but it's still not the great revealer that many believe.

Any undesirable traits in our children came from their other parent.

If the main reason why we research our past is to discover who we are, then it is not surprising that the implications of genetic research have become a fascination among many family historians in recent years. The fact that genetics may help prove or disprove who our ancestors are, or indicate that disparate family groups with the same surname do in fact all descend from the same pair of ancestors, is only part of this new area of interest. That we may now be able to know which of our traits and characteristics were passed on to us by ancestors now gone is an interesting prospect. And that we can now seriously consider what we might pass on to future generations could be a matter of considerable importance. At least, that is the theory.

According to one expert: "Knowing our genetic profiles can help us fulfill our desires to add lasting meaning to human life." However, that is probably doubtful. Nevertheless, many family historians are expanding their research to create family health histories that may point to disease-causing genes in their families.

Look on the Internet and you will find several firms advertising that they will undertake Ycs or mtDNA tests (or both) for a few hundred dollars. You can even receive a "Y-Line certificate, suitable for framing." However, using DNA to help trace your ancestry is currently not something that most will be able to take advantage of. Where it is already becoming of use is in confirming, or otherwise, that families living in different parts of the country, or in different countries around the world, and having the same or similar surname, do have a common ancestor.

Now for the science. Our bodies are made up of basic building blocks called cells. Each cell has a nucleus, which controls the cell's functions. Within the nucleus are two sets of chromosomes, 23 received from the mother and 23 from the father. Each chromosome is comprised of strings of DNA (deoxyribonucleic acid), which hold the blueprint (genome) of who we are. The DNA is arranged in the form of two strands wrapped together to resemble a twisted ladder or "double helix." These amino acid strings are made up of nucleotides that are given the letter names of A, C, T, and G (adenine, cytosine, thiamine, and guanine), connected to bases or the rungs of the ladder. It is the order of the letters that determines the color of our hair and eyes, our height, and our predisposition to certain diseases. In addition to nuclear DNA there is also genetic material found within the cytoplasm that surrounds the nucleus: mitochondrial DNA.

As we have inherited our DNA from all our ancestors, however distant, they share with us a portion of this information. The closer the relationship, the more similar our DNA will be. It is therefore possible, in theory, to

Defining idea... **"Genetics explains why you look like your father, and if you don't, why you should."**
HIGH SCHOOL EXAM ANSWER

establish family links among individuals and families and even tribes and other indigenous groups.

One-namers are among the heaviest users of the DNA test, hoping to link families across the world. See IDEA 41, *The truly obsessed.*

Try another idea...

Of the 23 pairs of chromosomes, 22 are similar, the father supplying one set and the mother the other. The 23rd pair determines the sex: a female has the 23rd pair made up of two X chromosomes, whereas a male has one X and one Y chromosome. Therefore, one of the 46 chromosomes in every male is a Y chromosome. This chromosome is passed almost unchanged from father to son, and any descendant strictly through the male line will have almost identical DNA on his Y chromosome as his ancestor. Therefore, distant cousins or those with the same surname can prove that they descend from the same male if they have the same Y chromosome DNA. It was this method that was used to show that President Thomas Jefferson had descendants through Sally Hemmings, one of his slaves.

Mitochondrial DNA (mtDNA) is transmitted from a mother to all her children, both male and female. But it is only passed on through the female line, and so stops with each son. Any individuals sharing mtDNA can therefore say that they descend from a common female ancestor strictly through the female line.

Claims that whereas family historians are only tracing their own family tree, the Human Genome Project is tracing that of humanity may seem far-fetched at the moment, but who can tell what the future will hold?

"Celibacy is not hereditary."
FIRST LAW OF SOCIOGENETICS

Defining idea...

How did it go?

Q **I had hoped that if I had a DNA test it might prove that I was descended from Abraham Lincoln, which is the family tradition. Is that not the case, then?**

A *It depends on whether you are boy or girl and if you think the descent is through males or females. If you can get a known descendant of the president to have a DNA test then you may be able to prove you share an ancestor. Otherwise, you may need to steal a bit of Washington's hair from a museum and get that DNA tested! Just don't believe everything you see on CSI.*

Q **What, then, can DNA testing be used for in tracing my past?**

A *DNA testing may help narrow research, a form of localization, but it is still a long way from proving who your ancestors were. This is an area of research where there will certainly be significant strides forward in forthcoming years.*

37

Digitize your data

You don't have to be swamped by scraps of paper. Get that scanner working overtime and let your computer take the strain.

Scanners are fun and very useful. Yes, there are some scanning techniques to learn, but once you've done it once or twice, it becomes rather easy.

Over the past thirty years, many people have proclaimed the imminent arrival of the paperless office. This was predicted to revolutionize the way we work, learn, and play—the work and education of the world would be converted into digital form, and lay the once popular paper medium to rest. However, along with the technology to facilitate the paperless office came the nemesis for those same predictions. This advance, known as the desktop printer, offered us the chance to use the theoretically obsolete paper to give us a permanent and easy-to-read copy of the information that we had purchased our computers specifically to store. Naturally, we obliged: we prefer not to have to read a large amount of text on a computer screen unless we really have to; a piece of paper is much easier to read, and can be

Here's an idea for you...

Many believe that they should always scan at the greatest possible resolution. Not so. We need to choose a scan resolution based on the output device that will process that image, normally a video monitor or a printer; and, if the latter, the size of the print. The math is complicated and incomprehensible to most, so experiment. Scan a good clean image at different resolutions–say at 72, 150, 300, 600, and 1,200 dpi. Then print them out at letter size on a good quality glossy paper and see the differences. Try smaller and larger print sizes. You will probably find 300 dpi is sufficient.

Defining idea...

"Try to be conspicuously accurate in everything, pictures as well as text. Truth is not only stranger than fiction, it is more interesting."
WILLIAM RANDOLPH HEARST
(1863–1951), newspaper publisher

taken to places that a computer has never even seen.

A large number of human beings regard computers as unreliable, and would not trust them with so much as a scrap of information unless they really had to. Nevertheless, there are very many really sensible reasons for creating digitized copies of your documents, photographs, ephemera, and the like. Security is only one of them, albeit an important one. The ability to share your information with others comes a close second, together with the fact that you can easily incorporate the images into your research notes, histories, and anything else you care to create.

A flatbed scanner is very much like a photocopier, to the extent that it has a glass plate under a lid, and a moving light that scans across under it. Like a photocopier, a scanner allows you to scan photos, paper documents, books, magazines, large maps, or even three-dimensional objects such as coins and medals. However, instead of creating another piece of paper, it creates an image in memory—a digital image, with which we can do as we please.

In addition to the scanner itself, we must use software to operate it. Some scanner software can operate independently, and some cannot. Most image editor programs, such as Adobe Photoshop or Corel's Paint Shop Pro, have a menu item allowing you to import a scan.

Scanned images are ideal for including in a scrapbook project. See IDEA 40, *Creative scrapbooking.*

Try another idea...

The actual scanning process can be as easy or as complicated as you want. There is a learning curve to climb before you will be producing scans worthy of the originals, but the effort will certainly be worth it.

If you do scan into an image-editing program, or open a previously scanned image, then you can crop it, adjust its contrast and brightness, and make other alterations. When the image is as you want it, you can either print it or write it to a disk or both. Always save you image as a TIFF file. Both TIFFs and JPGs are industry standard formats but there are distinct advantages to selecting the TIFF option, not least quality. This will result in significantly larger file sizes but will be worth it in the long run.

Last, remember copyright. The rules are complicated but there is a lot of information on the Internet. Also see *Carmack's Guide to Copyright and Contracts* for more detailed information.

"Life is not significant details, illuminated by a flash, fixed forever. Photographs are."
SUSAN SONTAG (1933–2005), author, critic

Defining idea...

How did it go?

Q How can I scan a document that is larger than the scanner bed?

A   *There are a few large (11 × 17 inch) flatbed scanners, but they are quite expensive. Otherwise, you can scan two or more partial images and join them. The manual way is to open the images in a photo program, and enlarge the canvas size of one image large enough to include the other part(s), and then copy them in. Use the layers option as it is then easier to align the various parts. Joining images this way is called stitching and some image editing programs include specific tools for stitching.*

Q I get odd patterns in the images I scan. What's the reason for this?

A   *If you're scanning printed material (books, magazines, newspapers, postcards) instead of original photographs, then what you are getting are moiré patterns, and this is to be expected. Magazine images are not at all the same thing as real photographs, as they are made up of thousands of tiny dots. When you undertake a scan you are imposing another matrix of dots and the two clash and produce a murky herringbone, crosshatched, or dotted pattern. To improve your images, always scan the original at least 600 dpi and then use the "descreen" option (present in most scanning software). With a little experimentation, much improved results are possible.*

38

Publishing on the web

Keep it to yourself if you want, but you can share the results of your sleuthing with the outside world using the Internet—and it's fun to do, too.

The Internet allows you to open the window to your family's history from the comfort of your own home.

Among the best of the online resources are all the people out there who you can contact via newsgroups, mailing lists, etc. Through them you can tap into a vast amount of information that you might not otherwise be aware of—the information that is not systematically indexed or filed anywhere, or that is at too great a distance to access directly.

If you have been researching your family history for a while and keeping a "research log" of what you have found where, the Internet is an ideal medium for you to share and circulate this information among others. The recent developments in new tools have made it easier for people to publish online, reducing the technological hurdles while increasing the breadth of options for publishing. So what are your options?

The term "mailing list" was originally applied to a collection of names and addresses used to send material to multiple recipients. The term now often includes the

Take the time to assess the information you have collected and decide on the best way to publish it for your purposes. Before you take any first steps, sample what's already on the Internet to see how it works. For instance, you might decide that you want to set up your own website so other family members can see the fruits of your efforts any time they wish.

people subscribed to such a list, so the group of subscribers are referred to as "the mailing list," or simply "the list." An individual can subscribe or unsubscribe themselves to any list. Mailing lists tend to be quite specialized and those within family history are usually aimed at members of a society at those with interests in a specific area, occupation, or specific surname.

A "newsgroup" is the electronic equivalent of a message board, with the facility for messages to be posted from many users in different locations. They are mostly used for messages asking for help and advice, or writing about topics you feel may be of interest to others. Newsgroups are technically distinct from, but functionally similar to, "discussion forums" on the web. Internet forums offer the additional capability to hold discussions. Web-based forums, which began around 1995, perform a similar function as the dial-up "bulletin boards" and Internet newsgroups that were numerous in the 1980s and '90s. A sense of virtual community often develops around forums that have regular users. There are forums for a huge number of different family history topics.

An "e-zine" is a regularly produced newsletter that is accessed electronically, either via a website or delivered as email. They were first developed during the 1980s. E-zines are typically tightly focused on a subject area

"Leave nothing for tomorrow which can be done today."
ABRAHAM LINCOLN (1809–1865)

such as an occupation or specific surname. Some family and local history societies publish e-zines to provide information of interest to their members. An individual can subscribe or unsubscribe themselves to receive a copy. E-zines are ideal to distribute among family members to give updates on the family history.

To help you in the task of properly organizing your information into a suitable format to get it online, look at IDEA 37, *Digitize your data*.

Try another idea...

"Blog" (short for *weblog* or *web log*) is the term used to describe an "online diary" or "journal." The blog format allows inexperienced computer users to make diary entries with ease. People blog poems, prose, complaints, daily experiences, family history, and more, often allowing others to contribute. These have really come to the fore since 2001. A blog site typically contains a list of links, or blogroll, to other blogs that the blog author reads or affiliates with. As a diary of your family history studies, it's a fantastic way to share your experiences with others or simply to create a record for yourself. The distinction between blogs and forums can be somewhat blurred.

A website is just a collection of individual files stored on a web server (computer), usually with permanent access to the Internet and usually accessed via a homepage with its own special address (URL). To date, it is estimated that there are over 80 million websites.

A word of caution, though: Do be mindful of privacy laws and common sense. In this age of identity theft and Internet crime, you should not publish items about living people, especially children, without consent. Take care to keep the subjects of your research protected.

"Curiosity is one of the most permanent and certain characteristics of a vigorous intellect."
SAMUEL JOHNSON (1709–1784), critic, poet, and lexicographer

Defining idea...

How did it go?

Q   How can I get people to create links to my website?

A   *It is essential that the information on your website is relevant, concise, well organized, and kept up-to-date so that people are going to want to link to it. Next look for other relevant local or family history websites that are going to attract the same type of person you think would be interested in visiting your website. Last, contact those sites' webmasters to ask if they would like to exchange links with you. Do bear in mind that many societies, archives, and commercial sites do have set policies as to what type of sites they will link to.*

Q   How can I tell which online publications contain trustworthy and reliable information and also make mine credible?

A   *Whatever publishing medium is being used, any information is only as good as the person who presents it. The Internet is no better or worse than any other method. However, the Internet does magnify the problem because of the vast amount of material that can be found online and the ease with which it can be duplicated and links created. Additionally, people don't always quote the source of any information—thus, it is not always easy to validate the source or check for any additional information. You need to record enough information so that another researcher can determine what you have actually searched. Remember: Without proof, there is no truth, so cite your sources and place more trust in others who do likewise.*

39

Grave responsibilities

Many cemeteries are places of outstanding historical interest, offering great insights into past times.

Having departed this mortal coil their remains ended up somewhere: potter's field to private cemeteries.

Though they are sometimes portrayed as a bit sinister or creepy, cemeteries are actually peaceful and often beautiful places. Visiting the final resting place of a distant relative can help you feel a connection to that person—and may yield some great details about her life.

The term "cemetery" comes from the Greek word *koimiteri*, meaning "sleeping places." The idea of landscaped public cemeteries came from Italy, France, and Sweden. The winding, tomb-lined avenues and well-contrived vistas of the landscaped cemetery at Pere-Lachaise in Paris were widely admired. It was this model and others like it that gave rise to the designed resting places we know today, complete with paths, trees, and flowers.

Cemeteries can be public or private, secular or religious, large or small, but all will have records that can be invaluable in your genealogical search. Public cemeteries are under the purview of the local government, and are funded by the taxpayers. As a public works entity, the records for public cemeteries are generally open to those who want to see them. Private cemeteries, on the other hand, are private businesses, and these are maintained by the fees collected for burial therein. Privacy laws and procedures may preclude these cemeteries from sharing records with you, but many are willing to help with specific genealogical research. Cemeteries affiliated with a specific religious institution can also be considered private, in that their upkeep is paid for by the fees collected for burial, though non-secular cemeteries are not necessarily for-profit businesses. Records for these cemeteries are held by the religious institution, but are often available for search.

Whatever type of cemetery your ancestor is buried in, records will be held by a sexton, who oversees the business of the cemetery, or at the town hall. The sexton will have burial registers, plot sale records, burial plot maps (called plats), and possibly even financial records that indicate who paid for the plot and its upkeep—all documents that will reveal information helpful to your research. **Burial registers** are chronological listings of who is buried in the cemetery. All will list the name, date of burial, and plot in which the deceased was buried; others may offer more personal details. **Plot sale records** will detail who bought the plot and when, and who is buried in the plot. Any fees associated with the upkeep of the gravesite will be included here. **Plot maps,** or plats, will show you where individual graves are and who owns them. Used in conjunction, these records will point you to family members who survived the ancestor in question and help you expand your family tree.

Here's an idea for you... **Find out if there are organized guided tours of your local burial ground. As an integral part of our heritage, they are extremely interesting places to visit and a knowledgeable guide will give you all sorts of pointers to the clues you should look for about historical funerary practices...**

It can sometimes be a bit difficult to figure out which cemetery your family member is buried in. Cemeteries change names and hands—even locations—over the years. Some cities have many nearby cemeteries. Some small towns use cemeteries that lie some distance from their borders. If you have an obituary, the burial information is often included there. If not, a quick search on the web will give you a listing of cemeteries in the area where your ancestor lived; phone calls to the sextons of the cemeteries will confirm whether or not your family member is interred there.

Finding the gravesite of a relative is a profound moment, one you will surely want to commemorate. Many people make rubbings of tombstones with paper and a fat crayon. If you want to do this, it's best to check with the sexton first, as rubbings can harm very fragile grave markers and some cemeteries prohibit the practice. To be safe, bring a camera and something to write the details of the headstone on.

Monuments and headstones are a great source of information. Epitaphs can be prolific or simple, but the vast majority includes, at the very least, the deceased's name and years of birth and death. They might also include the names of any other family members buried in the plot, nicknames, and clues about the deceased's life. "Loving wife, mother, and sister" is not an uncommon inscription, and even such a simple phrase can give you a better picture of the family member who rests there.

Once you have located the burial of your ancestor, why not see if you can discover an obituary in the local newspaper? Take a look at IDEA 9, *All the news that's fit to print*.

Try another idea…

"And, when he shall die, Take him and cut him out in little stars, And he will make the face of Heaven so fine, That all the world will be in love with night, And pay no worship to the garish sun."
WILLIAM SHAKESPEARE,
Romeo and Juliet

Defining idea…

How did
it go?

Q **Where do I find cemetery records?**

A *Cemetery records are generally still kept at the office on or near the site. The records usually give the name of the deceased, age, address, and occupation, the date of death and of burial, and the position of the grave. You should also be able to discover who else is buried in the same plot. If you are really lucky, this may include several generations of your family. (One of my family graves lists seventeen members of the extended family.) These cemetery records are arranged chronologically, and are not usually indexed alphabetically.*

Q **Among some family papers I have discovered a burial plot deed. Can you give me more information about this?**

A *Many families purchased a private plot for family burials. The family received a burial plot deed (proof of plot purchase) which needed to be shown at the cemetery when another burial was required in the plot. The deed should also include the plot number, allowing you to search in the cemetery grave book to discover who else is buried in the same plot. The cemetery may also hold plot records stating who originally purchased the plot and paid the burial fees.*

40

Creative scrapbooking

Have you ever thought of producing a book to pass down through the generations—a book of few words but many illustrations? It's well worth considering.

Get your artistic side into action and scrapbook the results of your research. Your imagination can run wild as you wield the glue gun and do crazy things with pinking shears.

If you have been wondering what you could leave behind for the generations to come, then perhaps a "heritage scrapbook" might be the answer. But where do you begin?

There are two important questions to answer from the outset. First, what do you want to scrapbook, and second, who do you want to give the scrapbook to, if anyone? And, if you are thinking that scrapbooking involves those large, cheap books that we used as kids, then think again. We are in another league here. All the rules about archival quality materials are obeyed. Scrapbooks—or to use the fancier

Here's an idea for you...

The story you are trying to tell isn't limited to photos and family trees and cold, hard facts. Include other information in your album. Family traditions, a sketch plan of a house you once lived in, newspaper clippings, pictures of tools of the person's trade, a map showing where the family originated, rubbings from gravestones. Experiment, make mistakes–it's fun. Enjoy.

term, "heritage albums"—can combine photos, annotations, drawings, newspaper clippings, mementos, and whatever your creative side can dream up.

So, what scrapbooking project might be suitable for a seeker of their past? Don't try to do a whole family tree—that would be crazy. Choose a particular person or family group, or what you know about your house, or your local watering hole, or the village, or your street, or a particular occupation, or a significant year, or … well, whatever you like. It might seem like a daunting task, but once you take that first step toward completing the first page of your first album, you'll be surprised at how easy it is.

Now you need to get organized. Once you have decided on your project—and start with something small if you haven't done this before—you need to gather together what you have and perhaps determine what you don't have so you can go scavenging. With all the elements at your fingertips, you'll get a clearer idea of what you want to say with the pages you're about to create. Sketch out a "storyboard," on the back of an envelope if you want, and then start arranging and rearranging the various pieces. You should have already been thinking about captions and some narrative text because you won't get away with just pictures. Don't worry if your handwriting is less than perfect—there are lots of different

Defining idea…

"To forget one's ancestors is to be a brook without a source, a tree without a root."
CHINESE PROVERB

computer fonts you can use, including some that look vaguely like handwriting.

In addition to the items you are going to scrapbook, you will need to get ahold of the pages,
to stick the bits and pieces to, and some "embellishments," as they are called. You can buy starter kits, which include an album, a few pages, and a selection of said embellishments. Look out for those aimed specifically at the heritage scrapbooker, but choose carefully because some of them are far from suitable. The great thing about scrapbooking is that you can throw out any of the rules about design you may read in any of the dozens of books on the subject, and just do your own thing. You can get some really good ideas from these books, or from the hundreds of related websites.

Another major decision to make is whether to use original items in your scrapbook, or copies of them. In some ways, if you scrapbook properly, then this can be as safe a place as anywhere to permanently house those valuable photographs, certificates, and the like. But your sensibilities might be with mine, which means that you should only be using copies—*good* copies; indistinguishable from the originals. The originals can then be securely held elsewhere in the best archival conditions. Using copies also means that you can crop photographs and produce other images at more sensible sizes. And if you make a mistake you can throw the copy away and start again.

If you are reading this, you obviously believe your past is important. Have no doubt—your family for generations to come will appreciate all the work that you put into creating your very own heritage scrapbooks.

Understand those photos you are scrapbooking, so they are truly in context–see IDEA 46, *Families in focus*.

Try another idea…

"Memories of our lives, of our works and our deeds will continue in others."
ROSA PARKS (1913–2005), civil rights leader

Defining idea…

179

How did it go?

Q **I keep hearing that scrapbooks should be kept simple. Doesn't that suggest a lack of creativity?**

A *Not at all. Keeping it simple will concentrate the focus on the photographs, documents, and ephemera. It also makes it easier to do. You shouldn't just look at other scrapbooks for ideas—snip ideas from any magazines or brochures that pass your way.*

Q **I'm a computer nerd. Can't I produce a virtual scrapbook so I can upload it to my website?**

A *Nothing nerdish about that ... well, not much anyway. No, there is nothing to stop you from producing scrapbook pages this way—many others already do, and it's a growing area. There are also lots of helpful scrapbook "supplies" that can be bought as digital versions. Or you can produce your own, of course.*

41

The truly obsessed

For some, gathering every reference to a particular surname or place is their raison d'être. It may not be your idea of fun, but don't knock them because they could help you.

People who have unusual surnames have often been intrigued by them and are now using modern technology to build up lists of everybody sharing those names across the world.

Cabbin, Caberry, Cabin, Cackett, Cad, Cadd, Caddell, Cadden, Caddle, Cade, Cadel, Cadell, Caden, Cadien, Cadle, Caide, Cake, Caket, Calenso, Calingham, Calinghelm, Calinhem, Callaff, Callangham, Callenso, Callingham, Calthorpe, Caltrup, and Calverley are just some of the subjects of one-name studies. Our names are one of the things that differentiate us from everyone else. As you start to exhaust your personal research and hit the proverbial brick wall you might think about widening the scope of your search and collecting all instances of a particular name (and its variances), perhaps even world-wide, then organizing them into family groups—a "one-name study." It provides the opportunity to continue with your interest in history, but with the hope that, one day, your elusive ancestors will be exposed. This does not, of course, have to be one of the surnames in your own lines—it could be that of a distant ancestor's husband or wife, or just a familiar name that grabs your imagination.

181

The gathering and in-depth study of a particular name can give you a fantastic insight into its distribution. Tracking back via genealogical methods will also show you all of the name's earliest variants.

There is a need for real commitment to undertake this type of study because it has a much wider scope and opens wide the ability to communicate with other researchers. If you choose to research a bloodline, you will eventually come into contact with cousins. They may be several generations removed but they are still cousins. It is challenging to be a specialist on your "name" and very rewarding to be able to help people to extend their own family trees. However, be warned: It is very absorbing and you will inevitably get side-tracked, fascinated by the history and events that surrounded and influenced these other families, perhaps even explaining why they immigrated, migrated, or emigrated.

A one-name study can also concentrate on particular aspects, such as geographical distribution of a name and the changes in that distribution over the centuries, or attempt to reconstruct the genealogy of as many lines as possible bearing that name. A common ambition is to try to identify the origins of the name, especially if it appears to derive from a place name, but for many names there will not be a single origin.

Here's an idea for you... **To discover more about your earlier ancestors, try delving into the extraordinary records of local libraries, which can reveal the history of communities in a variety of ways.**

Some researchers choose to transcribe and index original sources. Others use existing transcripts and contemporary lists, like trade directories, to collect information about the inhabitants of one place or one name. The clever researcher, however, will use any sources that are available to her. Some choose just to determine which records and indexes exist about their area—be they found in a book, on microfilm, on CD, or on the Internet—to help other researchers.

When dealing with larger amounts of information, proper data management is essential in order to allow good storage and retrieval. There's more on this in IDEA 19, *Files, formats, and family trees*, and IDEA 37, *Digitize your data*.

Try another idea...

People collect information on all sorts of things, creating databases of just about every class of record that might be of use to the family or local historian—everything from apprenticeship records to tax rolls, and from indexes of orphans to lists of vagrants. Many of these smaller specialized indexes have not been widely published but may be held by individuals or societies.

One-place studies can also be a very interesting avenue of research—collecting all information about the area where you live, came from, or from where your ancestors hailed. They are also a useful source for the rest of us for gaining more information about the places from which our ancestors originated. Organizing a one-place study can lead you to very specific and unusual sources for local and family history, by virtue of the fact that you are researching all the surnames within a given area. The amount of information you collate really depends on how far you want to go—your options are never ending...

"A fanatic is one who can't change his mind and won't change the subject."
WINSTON CHURCHILL (1874–1965)

Defining idea...

How did it go?

Q   How do I start a one-name study?

A   *You may find it useful to start by assessing how rare or common the name you are interested in is. You can look at its geographical distribution to determine just how big a task you are taking on. Some people choose to be selective and research names that are relatively rare; others are work-ing on larger studies with world populations of tens of thousands. You can then start collecting information on a systematic basis. Many of the initial sources you will use are the same as those used by other genealo-gists before spreading your wings in other directions to the more unusual sources. If someone is already doing a one-name study of your desired name, or even a one-place study, why not approach them and offer to join forces? It could be of massive benefit to us all.*

Q   Where can I locate information from one-name/one-place studies?

A   *Much of this information is now available not only on microfilm or micro-fiche but also on CD-ROM or the Internet. People often register their one-name or place-name study with the appropriate organizing body. There are also specialized publications outlining what indexes are being compiled and where you can find them.*

42

The Land Ordinance Act

The Bureau of Land Management holds records of more than 7 million land transactions in the United States, dating back to the age of Manifest Destiny.

In 1785, the Continental Congress passed the Land Ordinance Act, allowing the federal government to survey and sell for profit the so-called public domain lands lying west of the Ohio River.

When the Revolutionary War ended, the US government found itself with reclaimed land—and a lot of debt—on its hands. As a means of paying down the debt and populating the hard-won land, Congress passed the Land Ordinance Act, which gave the Treasury Department the power to sell land to settlers.

"Be it ever so humbug, there's no place like home."

NOEL COWARD (1899–1973),
actor, composer, and playwright

Surveyors were sent to the Public Domain territory—then comprised of Ohio, Indiana, Illinois, Michigan, Florida, Wisconsin, Alabama, Mississippi, Louisiana, Minnesota, Iowa, Missouri, and Arkansas—to take stock of the land. Their extensive **field notes** became the land records and established the legal boundaries of the United States. A similar process was undertaken when the Louisiana Purchase added another 500 million acres to the American map. Thousands of volumes of notes were generated by the surveyors, and they are now held in the archives of the BLM, filed geographically by state.

When a piece of land was sold, a **land patent** was issued. Completely different from an inventor's patent, a land patent was the deed between the US government and the land purchaser. Upward of 5 million patents are now held by the BLM, all numbered successively and filed numerically. An extensive discussion of land patents can be found at the BLM's website, at www.glorecords.blm.gov/visitors/patents.asp.

"Well! Some people talk of morality, and some of religion, but give me a snug little property."

MARIA EDGEWORTH (1767–1849),
The Absentee

Tract books were also used to track land sales. These records are somewhat simplified, outlining who bought what land when. Tract entries were sent to the Land Office, which then generated the official land patent. These original documents are also housed by the BLM, as are microfilm versions of some records.

To learn more about researching with deeds, go to IDEA 43, *In deed*.

Try another idea...

The BLM is currently working to make their millions of documents available to visitors on the web. Thousands of document images, dating as far back as 1820, are available to search, with more documents being added every day. To access the digital archives, get updates on available documents, and to learn more about the history of America's expansion, visit the BLM's website at www.glorecords.blm.gov/.

Q   **Is there anywhere else I can find information about a particular property I have discovered in these records?**

A   *This is where a local history library may be able to help considerably. There you may find photographs of the area or other illustrations. Don't forget to look for postcards as well. On the local level, check the county offices for deeds, survey maps, tax records, and building plans.*

43

In deed

Deeds, the legal records of property transfer between individuals, are an easily accessible and endlessly helpful source of information about your ancestors.

If your ancestor was a landholder, there is probably a deed record for the property tucked away in his county courthouse. A quick trip to the courthouse or archive may be all you need to jump-start your search.

Deeds record the sale of land from one individual to another, as opposed to grants, which record the sale of land from a government to an individual. Deed records are quite helpful for the amateur genealogist, since they exist for so many of our ancestors and because they can contain so many details about their lives.

If you know where your ancestor's land was located, visit the jurisdiction's courthouse. Once there, your first step is to find the deed indexes. These indexes are the key to navigating the bewildering amount of land records. The indexes will be sorted by grantor (or "sellor"), buyer (or "grantee"), or sometimes both. Names will

Here's an idea for you... **There is every likelihood that where you now live was once farmland—and, if not you, then perhaps where your parents or grandparents lived. So, while you are in the library or record office see what else they have for those parcels of land that were part of your past.**

be listed in alphabetical order or grouped by letter, though the entries may not be listed chronologically. The indexes themselves can be quite helpful, as they often contain details pertinent to the sale, like names, dates, and locations. On a more functional level, they will also point you to the volume and page of the deed book where your family member's entry appears.

With the entry location in hand, you can request a copy from the county clerk's office or view the microfilm version at your local library or nearest Family History Center. Note that the deed book will contain only the details of the land transaction, not the deed itself. (Original deeds were and are retained by the purchaser.) Those details will tell you much about your family member and his life, however. You will find the names of the seller and buyer, the date of the transaction, the location of the land, and the amount of money paid for the land. If you're lucky, there might even be notations about occupations, spouses, and witnesses. There will also be an in-depth description of the land itself, including boundaries and physical characteristics.

Not only can a deed record help you pinpoint your relative at a specific point in time, it can also direct you to more sources. Check census returns, newspapers, tax records, vital records, and city or town directories from the area for mention of your relative and his family. Also, many archives and libraries hold historic regional maps; see if you can find one from the time your family member resided on the land.

As a source for local and family genealogists, land deeds are of great value and present an enormous database of land ownership and usage. For more on using this source to best advantage, see Patricia Law Hatcher's *Locating Your Roots.*

Farmland was what comprised most of the country's manors. Find out more about land ownership going back centuries from IDEA 32, *Manors maketh man*.

Try another idea…

"A farm is an irregular patch of nettles bounded by short-term notes, containing a fool and his wife who didn't know enough to stay in the city."
S. J. PERELMAN (1904–1979), humorist and screenwriter

Defining idea…

191

How did it go?

Q **What about land records for homesteaders?**

A *The Homestead Act of 1863 drove America's Westward expansion with the promise of free land and a chance to stake one's claim on the frontier. The Act provided that anyone could have 160 acres of land, free of charge, if, at the end of five years, the land had a house, a well, some fence, ten plowed acres, and people living on it. As you might imagine, many young Americans took advantage of this opportunity and moved West. Many land records have been indexed, and are available through the Bureau of Land Management (www.glorecords.blm.gov/visitors/).*

44

Bricks and mortar

The architectural heritage of the United States is rich and varied. Even your own home will have a story to tell about the history of your area.

Look around the streets of any city or town and you'll discover that there is a wide variety of treasures to behold. From large country houses, churches, or cathedrals to humble houses, each has its special place in our past.

An examination of the architectural evidence and the style in which a house was built and the materials used can indicate the approximate age of the construction. It is important to remember that since time began people have been improving and extending their properties, so building may have occurred over a considerable number of years.

One of the first things to look at is where the house is built. Development tended to start near the center of a community. The original plot may have subsequently been

Here's an idea for you... **To discover what your home looked like prior to you taking up residence, check for any photographs. Ask previous occupants, neighbors, local or family history societies. Also check for any events—such as a street party for Fourth of July, a St. Patrick's Day parade, a summer barbecue, etc.—during which your street or house might have been photographed.**

subdivided, so a plot of land that originally had just one dwelling on it may now have two or three.

Look at the type, style, and size of any bricks used. These were often stamped with the name of the maker, which again may hold clues because you can pinpoint when they were in production. However, in older properties when extending or renovating it is now common practice to use recycled bricks to try to match the originals, so beware. If you have a cellar, pay it special attention because this is likely to define the original construction.

Examine the roof space. Can you see single brick spaces in the walls? These would have been used as "keys" for wooden scaffolding long before the advent of modern metal pole scaffolding. Look at the style of the beams and structure within the loft space—the styles changed over the years as different building methods developed. Look at what the actual roofing material is, but bear in mind that the roof may have been replaced at some time. Also look at the roofs on nearby buildings. What were the local building materials? Was it local tiles or slates?

Look at the chimney stacks and how they relate to the fireplaces within the property. Are they original or were they added at a later date? If they have been removed is there evidence of what previously existed?

If your property is a timber-framed house, see how much timber has been used in the exterior and is showing. The closer the beams, the more money spent on wood, giving an indication of the social standing of the original owners.

What do you do when there are no photographs available for the house or other particular building that interests you? How do you discover what it was like? See Idea 45, *Plots and plans*.

Try another idea…

Design and tastes change over time, and this will be reflected in the internal structure of your home. The windows and door frames can give tell-tale clues about the evolution of your house. The shape/type of windows and the keystones above them can all give an indication of age. If you do not have original windows and door frames, try to look at the other properties on your street for clues.

The staircase can be one of the oldest features in a house, and in older or higher-status buildings one of the central structures. Look for any carvings or decorations, along with any exposed wood or paneling, all of which can indicate the age of a property.

It is unlikely that any original decoration survives. However, remnants of past decoration may be found hidden away in the corners of closets. Diaries and insurance records, particularly fire insurance claims, contain listings and descriptions of houses and their contents. Probate inventories may list the deceased's belongings on a room-by-room basis. A number of publications are available should you want to discover more about the internal aspects of a property and original decoration styles.

"We shape our buildings; thereafter they shape us."
WINSTON CHURCHILL (1874–1965)

Defining idea…

195

**Q   We live in a fairly new house–built in the 1990s–so it doesn't
have a lot of history. Is there anything of potential interest we
could look into?**

*A   You could take a look at what was there before your home was built.
Particularly if you live in an urban area, there may have been houses or
factories or workshops on that site previously. Ask your older neighbors
what they know or remember about the area—you may be surprised exactly
what people do know. Check out earlier photographs of the area. Sources
for these include local history societies, newspapers, and commercially
produced books, and, of course, the Internet.*

**Q   When trying to determine the true age of a property, what are
the pitfalls?**

*A   A building can often be constructed on the site of an earlier building. This
may be the result of the loss of the older building through neglect, to opti-
mize commercial potential, or to improve on the standard of housing in an
area. Many rebuilt structures incorporate material from an earlier building
that might suggest that the main structure is older than it really is. Often
building styles continued in an area even though the national trend was
different. Conversely, many modern buildings are constructed in an older
style (sometimes with reclaimed materials), which can make a property
appear older than it really is. It is important to cross-reference documentary and architectural evidence to minimize these risks.*

45

Plots and plans

In the absence of photographs, there are many other records that will give you a strong flavor what your house, or other particular building of interest, was like in the past.

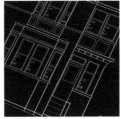

One of the main attractions of house history is that it combines many disciplines, requiring you to unearth clues about the lives of former inhabitants and discover more about the local community.

A good way to begin your quest is by asking your neighbors what they know about your house or street. Also look for printed histories of the area. Try to locate any surviving title deeds and conveyance documents relating to the house. If you don't have a mortgage, then you may already have them; otherwise, check the county clerk's office for land or property records. These will give a description of the house, its position, plot dimensions, names of previous owners and occupants, and details of transactions and mortgage and the date of construction.

Many local record offices produce information leaflets detailing how to trace the history of a house located in their area using their record holdings. Make sure you check this out before starting your research because it can save you a great deal of time and effort.

Today, all municipalities require developers to submit plans for approval prior to the commencement of building. The resulting building plans allow you to see what the original or intended layout of the house was, plus you can also follow any subsequent changes to a property over the years. Often the plans also show the various elevations of a property— enabling you to see what the building looked like even in the absence of photographs. You can find building site plans and blueprints in the local zoning office or the county clerk's office.

In the absence of blueprints or other records, you can also determine approximately when your house was built by seeing when it first appears on survey maps. By consulting consecutive editions, it is possible to track the development of an individual building, including any alterations and changes in use and plot size. The Library of Congress holds many historical land ownership maps and atlases; these may also be found in the archives on the county level.

Property assessment records, again held at the county level, are another rich source of information about a piece of property and its owner. These records give the names and addresses of owners and householders, details of the property, and the value assigned to that property. Taxes are based on these assessments, which offer you another avenue to explore. You can use tax records and returns, found on the county level, to trace property through the tax liability of the occupants.

If you wish to find out more about individuals, this can be done via information from birth, death, and marriage certificates; parish registers; census listings; wills; death records; electoral registers and poll books; telephone directories; newspapers; journals; and magazines.

Investigating the history of your house is an exciting and informative discipline, bringing you into direct contact with the past. Most of the records involved are easily accessible and can be found in your local archives. Your research can become as detailed as you want, combining local history and genealogy. And more important, it's really fun!

Try another idea...

For more information about how to examine the more permanent features of your home and start your own home survey, look through IDEA 44, *Bricks and mortar.*

Defining idea...

"A doctor can bury his mistakes but an architect can only advise his clients to plant vines."
FRANK LLOYD WRIGHT
(1867–1959), architect

How did it go?

Q   I don't have time to research the history of my home right now but what can I do to preserve the information and memories that I have?

A   *It is important to try to preserve all types of history. One of the things that you could do is to share the older pictures of your home with the local historical society or local history library if they don't already have copies. If you can, date the pictures and give a brief description and background to them. The many local history groups throughout the United States can offer you an enormous amount of help and advice and they publish a variety of books and journals relating to the communities they cover.*

Q   I know that my house is about one hundred years old but I am struggling to find it in earlier records. Why is that?

A   *Remember that names or numbers of houses are not always given, particularly in earlier records. With increased development, the street may have been renumbered or even renamed. Thus, 1 Main Street may now be 25 Spruce Road. Although all the houses in a road may look alike from the outside, they may have been built over a period of perhaps 20 years, and not in order, resulting in some numbers being left out. Registers recording these alterations may occasionally be found with the records of the local authority. The actual boundaries of a town will also have changed with time.*

46

Families in focus

Discovering old family photographs is enormously satisfying, but what do you actually see? Open your mind to *all* of what they are really telling you.

Photographer Diane Arbus wrote, "A photograph is a secret about a secret. The more it tells you the less you know." She was more than right, too.

Anyone researching their past will start by scouring their own homes, and those of relatives, for any family memorabilia. For most, of all the family documents we hope to uncover, none are more exciting in their discovery than photographs of ancestors whose likenesses before that moment were quite unknown.

Before the introduction of wide-scale photography in the 1850s, the production of visual images was in the hands of painters and draftsmen. Their skills necessarily included the ability to flatter and deceive. However, the idea that the camera cannot lie is far from true. Kafka called the camera a "mechanical mistake-thyself." As with all aspects of research you must be prepared to question the evidence.

Here's an idea for you... **Look again at your collection of old, and perhaps not so old, photographs. It is difficult, but try to put aside the passion they frequently instill. Ask a friend what they think they see before you explain who the people are and what they mean to you. The great-uncle you hated all your life, because he refused to take you fishing when you were five, may in fact have been quite a nice old guy, and someone else may see that in him.**

Defining idea... *"Photographers deal in things which are continually vanishing and when they have vanished there is no contrivance on earth which can make them come back again."*
HENRI CARTIER-BRESSON
(1908–2004), photographer

First you need to remember that the photograph performed quite a different function then than it does today. We have moved from the time when the sole purpose was to record a likeness or event for posterity—as the paintings that came before did—to a time when we click away like there is no tomorrow. Photography now, as Susan Sontag puts it, is as commonplace as "sex and dancing." In the early days, photographers were all professionals or very skilled amateurs. They were very much in control and frequently wanted to communicate some particular thought or emotion with their work.

Albert Einstein knew a thing or two about relatives as well as relativity: "A photograph never grows old. You and I change, people change all through the months and years, but a photograph always remains the same. How nice to look at a photograph of mother or father taken many years ago. You see them as you remember them. But as people live on, they change completely. That is why I think a photograph can be kind." Unfortunately, what Einstein left out of the equation—he knew something about equations, too—is that as we change so do our memories, warped by time and experience. Too often we see what we want to see. Family photographs don't change, but the stories we tell about them just might. Two people looking at the same photograph rarely see the same thing, particularly if they both knew the person concerned and had different experiences with them.

It is not only portrait-style family photographs that we need to be careful about. Many images of people at work or going about their daily business were carefully posed to put them in their very best light and to create an artistic composition. The images in collections held in local archives across the country also need to be very carefully scrutinized. Always ask yourself the question, Why? Why was that particular photograph taken? Why that view at that time?

Also be wary of rogue photos in your collection: not family or friends at all. Just as now, in the old days tens of thousands of celebrity photographs were sold, including royalty, actors and performers, and others on the then A list. If you cannot identify that little old lady, it might just be Florence Nightingale.

Undeniably, photographs are the most exciting of all the documents we collect. Some of us are luckier than others in the numbers we have, but we all cherish the memories they keep alive. Whether they really give an insight into an ancestor who we never actually knew is debatable.

Photos have a unique value, look after them. To develop your collection, see IDEA 49, *Cameras are not just for vacations!*

Try another idea...

"It takes a lot of imagination to be a good photographer. You need less imagination to be a painter because you can invent things."
DAVID BAILEY (1938–),
photographer

Defining idea...

How did it go?

Q   I have several old photos but I have no idea who they are. They are quite small, the size of a credit card, and stuck on card. Does this format come from a particular era?

A   *What you have are probably* cartes de visite, *which were introduced in 1860. The clues you need to look for include: the name and address of the photographer (usually on the back)—trade directories will tell you when he was in business there; the backdrop—these changed with time; fashion details—the actual clothes can be misleading as these could be worn for many years, because of hand-me-downs, so look at hairstyles and accessories, which were easily changed. There are lots of books that will help you with these last two.*

Q   Why does everyone look so miserable in old photographs?

A   *There is a belief that this was because of the long exposures needed and the various contraptions that were used to stop people from moving. The truth is quite different. Simply, you were not expected to smile when you had your picture taken—it was not what you did and to do so was unacceptable and would spoil the photograph.*

47

Places in perspective

Many elements of the landscape are invisible. Recognize the clues, though, and you'll discover your surroundings far beyond your normal pedestrian point of view.

Whether you live in a rural community, a small town, or a large suburb, its history will have followed the pattern of open field to enclosed land to village to town to city.

Wherever you now live, this pattern of change is often still visible and will almost certainly have been recorded in some way. Man's creation of the present-day urban and rural landscape has been a long process. As far back as the Neolithic period, people were busy clearing land for cultivation and grazing, and for establishing settlements.

Documentary sources will provide the greatest amount of material for study and any investigations should start at the local history library to see what relevant material has already been published. Documents are not the only source, though. There is an enormous amount of information stored in the buildings and the land itself, which can give up its secrets to the inquisitive mind and an educated eye.

Here's an idea for you...

Once you have identified a lost feature from the landscape on a map or in a published local history— whether it is a deserted village, a significant building, or estate now broken up, or the bar that used to be at the end of the road—your search has only just begun. You then need to discover if any evidence remains on the ground. So, with map and camera, set off to see what you can find. Leave the shovel at home—that's for the real experts. Some features may be obvious, others less so. Probably the boundary will still be recognizable, its "extent" now defining something else: separating the housing estate from the superstore. Perhaps there may be the remains of a wall or garden. The features you noticed from an aerial photograph may be invisible at ground level, but that in itself is a discovery.

At the local history library, start by actually asking for help. The knowledge held in the heads of most local archivists is quite incredible, certainly they usually know their collections inside out and will probably be able to point you to the right sources without searching catalogs. Initially look for any visual evidence of the changing face of the street, village, parish, or town—old postcards, drawings, photographs, watercolors.

Maps and plans are undoubtedly the sources of most use at this stage and will tell you more. The purpose is to identify what now remains of those ancient boundaries, or field names, or names of those owners or occupants of the roads and estates around us now.

Sometimes aerial photography is used to identify features in the landscape that cannot be seen from the ground. When the sun is low in the sky and shadows are more marked, features can be identified. Crop marks are also used, variations in the color and intensity occurring where the earth was disturbed, even many centuries ago.

I had a colleague who once said perspective was when you thought things disappeared but really they didn't. In a strange way, perhaps he was right.

To find out more about how to get the most from maps and plans, go through IDEA 17, • *Try another idea...* ***How does the land lie?***

"That series of inventions by which man from age to age has remade his environment is a different kind of evolution—not biological, but cultural evolution ..." *Defining idea...*
JACOB BRONOWSKI (1908–1974), historian and mathematician

207

How did it go? Q **I'm quite interested in the industries that were in the area where I now live. What sort of evidence might I find about them?**

A *There is a great deal that remains from early industries that deserves recording and preserving. At one end you have the artifacts that were produced: the pots, the drainage pipes, the cast-iron grates, and so forth. At the other end you have the factories, the mines, the workshops, and the machinery that produced the goods. The sources for researching industrial archaeology are the same: published research, maps and plans, and the archives of the companies themselves, which may survive in the local record office.*

48

A rue with a view

See your street and community through the eyes of those residents of earlier times by discovering contemporary postcards of the area. They provide a fascinating snapshot of the past.

It is difficult to adequately describe or illustrate the streets on which our ancestors walked or the churches where they were baptized, married, or buried. Postcards can paint those pictures.

Postcards had their origins in "message cards," which were introduced in Europe in the 1820s and were mailed with an envelope. In 1861, John P. Charlton patented the postcard, or "souvenir cards" as they were known, in the United States. By 1870, postcards were also being produced in Europe.

After promotional postcards advertising the World's Columbian Exposition held in Chicago in 1893 kicked off a national postcard craze, the US Postal Service issued "penny postcards," which could be sent for—that's right—just a penny.

The "divided back" postcard we're familiar with today came into use in the United States around 1907, though the format had been in use in Britain since 1902. Cheap and reliable, postcards rapidly became the medium for transmitting short messages to friends and family, and were used very much as we use email, texting, and telephones today. Millions of postcards were sent through the postal system every week, with a high proportion winding up in someone's album, only to be rediscovered many years later. Recognizing the value for posterity and sentimentality, people also started to buy postcards to keep as souvenirs, rather than just using them for communication.

World War I changed the emphasis of the subjects featured and also impeded the influx of the preferred German-printed postcards. With the introduction of the telephone, the use of picture postcards began to decline, never to really regain the same sort of use or popularity. Fewer types of cards were published as most firms involved in postcard production either changed direction or simply stopped trading. Postcards were relegated to something just sent to family and friends when you went on vacation.

Here's an idea for you... **Try collecting postcards of the same view of an area, taken over a number of years. This will allow you to compare and contrast the scenes and see just how the area has changed.**

Postcards began to regain popularity as an advertizing and art medium in the 1970s, and today they can be found in trendy stores, cafés, and entertainment venues. Since the 1950s, old postcards have become collectable items, a "must have" for a growing number of people.

So where are the best places to locate post-cards? Postcards can be found at local history, family history, book, and stamp fairs; antique and second-hand shops; garage sales; and from the various online auction sites. Another valuable source, of course, are family members—you never know what asking them might reveal.

For another "view" of the landscape, looking at those aspects that are invisible within a straightforward photograph, see IDEA 47, *Places in perspective*.

Try another idea...

There are many postcard clubs, catering to local and specialty interests. There is also a Postcard Index, a collection of thousands of postcards dating from the 1890s up to 1950 indexed by the recipient's name, address, and date that may help you locate postcards relevant to your family.

Nothing can compare with the information that you can obtain from a postcard and the way it can cater to all interests. Whether you're interested in a particular subject or interested in the events and fashions or social history of the past century, the postcard encapsulates it all.

"Life is a great big canvas, and you should throw all the paint on it you can."
DANNY KAYE (1913–1987), stage, film, and television entertainer

Defining idea...

How did
it go?

Q   How much can I expect to pay for a postcard?

A   *Even quite old cards can cost under $1, though the best street scenes can cost much more. Pictures of churches are very reasonably priced. For special subject cards (such as the Titanic, suffragist, and baseball teams), you can pay over $100, while ordinary themes (flowers and country views) can be quite cheap. Generally, the card's age doesn't provide an indication of cost: A card from the 1970s may sell for more than one from the turn of the century for instance. As with stamp collecting, you should only start collecting postcards for illustrating your family or local history or because you like the subject matter, and not for possible financial gain—it is very easy to lose money by attempting to collect for profit.*

Q   I've been given an album containing old picture postcards. How can I discover more about them?

A   *If the postcards are not too tightly glued into the album see if you can carefully remove them without damaging any. Take a really close look at the picture itself, to determine any special relevance to your family (e.g., Is it a picture of people or places that you recognize?). Looking at the rear side, the stamp, postmark, message, and address can tell you something about the sender and the recipient. Do you recognize the address to which it was posted? Does the message make reference to your family or their friends or hometown?*

49

Cameras are not just for vacations!

Or, how to make sure you create your own modern-day photo archive.

Perhaps it's time to reevaluate and even return to some of the reasons our ancestors created the photographs they did.

In the days before television, digital pictures, and the mass media, family photographs and the recording of place and time had a significance and meaning that we have possibly lost, to our own and our descendants' detriment. Every day, millions of images are forced at us from books, magazines, and newspapers, through advertising, and the Internet, and in brochures and on packaging. On the whole, our own efforts pale into insignificance compared with all that is around us. And this, in spite of the fact that we take more and more and more pictures of our own every year.

Perhaps it is all too easy now. With the digital revolution, taking pictures is cheap: effectively free once you have the camera, or the mobile camera-phone. There's no

Here's an idea for you...

Choose a photograph from your family album or take your own photograph or series of photographs: a person or group, your town, your house, people at work. Now, why did you take, choose, or identify that particular image? What is it that might be of interest to future generations, not necessarily your own family's? An archive is for the future but of the present. Do your choices match those needs?

Defining idea...

"A family's photograph album is generally about the extended family and, often, is all that remains of it."
SUSAN SONTAG (1933–2005),
author and critic

need for film, no need for processing, and the results are more or less instantaneous. The considered portrait or the carefully judged streetscape are mostly from the past or from today's professionals, and even they are now more interested in artistic merit than a record of reality. Photos are great, they capture the moment and in many ways benefit from a bit of proverbial roughness round the edges: There is a certain truth, an honesty, there.

Your photo archive for today needs to include the impetuous moments but, more important, it needs to include simple, honest, straightforward portraits: of ourselves, our family, our home, and our surroundings. As this is an archive for the future, the images need to be fully captioned: who they are of, where they are from, when they were taken, plus any other relevant details: "on her seventieth birthday"; "before the house was pulled down"; "Millie's cousin." If only our families had done just that in the past. How often do we hear, "I have all these photos but I don't know who they are of"?

Think, too, about a three- or even four-generation photograph. In fact, many of the best family photographs involve more than one person: The natural reaction between mother and child, grandma and grandpa, brother and sister is hard to cover up. Like so much in life, simplicity should be the overriding principle, so forget complicated backdrops and props. Take a look in a few professional photographers' shop windows for ideas, or in the glossy magazines.

By collecting postcards of a specific place you can create a unique archive. Learn more from IDEA 48, _A rue with a view._

Try another idea...

With the ease of taking photos has come the ability to seamlessly alter the content of a photograph and create a lie. Photo-manipulation programs allow you to do all sorts of wonderful things: remove blemishes, create graduation photos of those who never went to college, remove unwanted relatives from wedding groups, and even add those who weren't there at all. Such an image is fake, it's a lie; it ceases to be a true record; it ceases to be any sort of record.

There is an argument that formal photographs tend to make us look at the subjects rather than into them, and that is a bad thing. Candid images need something to counterbalance them, without the overtones of emotion. Don't stop snapping away and capturing those irreplaceable moments. They have a very important place in our culture and our memories.

"You need to learn to see and compose. The more time you waste worrying about your equipment the less time you'll have to put into creating great images. Worry about your images, not your equipment."

KEN ROCKWELL, photographer

Defining idea...

How did
it go?

Q **Surely the "formal" photograph can be as atypical as any other photograph. If I get my family to go out of their way to dress up and get their hair done specially, then this isn't really them either, is it?**

A *Quite right. The one major difference between what we need to do now and what our ancestors did is that we should remain as natural as possible. If you are usually seen in shirt and tie, then wear them; if jeans and T-shirt, then those. The purpose is to capture an accurate likeness. The Victorian idea of not smiling was not so crazy—we don't all go around with a supercilious grin on our faces all the time, do we?*

Q **I have tried taking a formal photo or two, but my family looks very self-conscious. I suppose it's because they are not used to it. Any suggestions?**

A *You could of course get a professional to do the work for you. Or you could follow the words of advice given as far back as 1849 by Henry Snelling: "The conformation of the sitter should be minutely studied to enable you to place her or him in a position the most graceful and easy to obtain. The eyes should be fixed on some object a little above the camera, and to one side but never into, or on the instrument, as some direct; the latter generally gives a fixed, still, staring, scowling, or painful expression to the face."*

50

Diversify—do your own thing

There are plenty of opportunities to follow your own interests and keep your passion burning. Research what really fascinates you, not what the books tell you you should be doing.

For many family historians, completing a family tree is only just the beginning. To just collect names and dates can be a very mundane and sterile activity.

Your ultimate goal should be to gain information and understanding about your ancestors and the lives they led, firmly setting them into their own special place in history with the locations and time periods in which they lived. But that doesn't mean you can't also search out anything that piques your interest along the way.

It's important to allow yourself the freedom to study anything that captures your imagination. Family historians are very much like any other detectives, piecing together clues, avoiding taking things for granted or at face value, dispelling myths, but in the meantime building up a detailed picture of the who, why, what, where, and when.

Here's an idea for you... **If you want to reach out to those interested in the same areas of research as yourself, try creating your own e-zine or blog (online diary). You could also circulate them to friends and family to keep them abreast of your latest findings.**

This is a journey that can take you in any direction and as far as you desire—depending on exactly what your goals and objectives actually are and your appetite for the chase down the road of discovery. So what are your options and how can you realize them?

After a time, many of us become "sidetracked" in our research, even if it's just a small diversion down a particular line of research to confirm a particular family story. You may want to discover if Bing Crosby was truly related to your father's family (as the story goes) or whether Great-Uncle Albert really did go to to Australia, and if he left any descendants on the way, and how many wives he had (at the same time).

You might have a major change of direction, caused by the fact that you cannot find your great-great-great-grandfather who was born in the 1780s. Not to be defeated, you decide to collect information on everyone of that particular surname anywhere in the world—starting your very own one-name study. Or, of course, you may discover that as you move back in time the majority of your ancestors came from a specific place for which there doesn't seem to be very much documented information, so you may decide to do a one-place study. This may, of course, be the place that you now live in but with no actual relevance to your ancestry.

Many of your ancestors may have been in the Army or Navy or been tinkers, tailors, or spies, but what did they actually do? What did their daily work involve? Perhaps military or naval history has grasped your imagination. Or do you want to join the ranks of those organizing specialized indexes of combmakers, lacemakers, gamekeepers, bricklayers, or rat catchers and the like?

Perhaps you want to help other people with their research by becoming involved in a local or family history society. If there isn't one in your local area, see if anyone is interested in helping you organize a group. Or do you want to get involved in transcribing and indexing records—for example, tax records or gravestones; newspapers with their obituaries, scandal, announcements, advertizements, sales particulars, and so forth?

If your interests are growing in the role of your ancestors in the military, take a look at IDEA 25, *Uncle Sam wants you!*

Try another idea…

"Imagination is a quality given a man to compensate him for what he is not, and a sense of humor was provided to console him for what he is."
OSCAR WILDE (1854–1900)

Defining idea…

Or you could do a historical survey of your house, or an ancestor's house, or trace its history, researching the families that lived there and how they fitted into the history of the area or into your history. You might be interested in the development of education in an ancestor's village—perhaps you might like to help compile the history of your ancestor's school (if one's not been written already).

Researching your family history and honing your research skills can lead you to look beyond the family tree, exploring much further than discovering just who you think you are.

Q **Why is it so important to make sure that I fully document my research?**

How did it go?

A *Properly documenting and taking time to organize a research log, setting down when and where you found your information, will save time and effort later in your research. Without doing this, you are likely to look at those same sources again, only to find, or not find, what you already knew. One of the first things suggested to new researchers is to check "what's been done before." Documentation can help avoid duplication of research, especially when several people are researching the same lines. We make use of transcripts and indexes and thus depend on high-quality previous research to help us. Without documentation, we do not know what sources somebody has used and therefore what we are looking at. Remember: "Without proof, there is no truth."*

Q **I'm interested in doing some research using some old colonial records—which I'm not able to read. Where do I go from here?**

A *Seeking out the assistance of a professional genealogist can be prudent if you encounter a challenging research problem like this. They also know exactly where to locate specific records, and what they contain. A professional assessment of your "case" can save a lot of time, and often money. It's especially useful where the documents you require are not easy for you to access. See the Association of Professional Genealogists (www.apgen .com) and the Board for Certification of Genealogists (www.bcgcertification .org) for more information.*

221

51

Start your search engines

The Internet is a vast collection of information and it grows remorselessly by the day, by more than a million pages. To get the best from it, you need to learn to use it effectively.

One of the greatest misconceptions people have when beginning to undertake research online is the belief that it will all appear at a click or three of their mouse.

The Internet is the largest repository of information in the world. And that is also its downside. Locating the valuable information that is out there to help us research our past can be a formidable task, particularly because as the amount of information grows, so do the number of "hits" when we undertake any search.

Searching the Internet is like searching for the proverbial needle. However, remember that there are various ways to search the content of the Internet and you can waste a lot less time chasing dead ends if you learn how to search more efficiently.

Search engines are the card indexes of the Internet—searchable databases of websites collected by special programs called crawlers, spiders, or robots. These scour the Internet and index the text they contain into a very large database. There are

Here's an idea for you...

Normally, when undertaking searches in online databases, less is more. In other words, you enter as little information as possible and only if there are too many results do you enter some additional data, and so forth, until the number of hits becomes manageable. It's the same with search engines, although here you will almost certainly have to start with a considered string of information. Try it. Just enter the name of an ancestor or place that interests you and note the number of hits. Then add some other relevant information: a town, an event, a subject such as "history" or "genealogy." Try different combinations and some Boolean operators to see how the number of hits is affected and, hopefully, you'll become more centered on what you want.

many such search engines and each has different strengths when searching for different types of information. Among the more powerful search engines for research purposes are Google (www.google.com), FASTSearch (www.alltheweb.com), Alta Vista (www.altavista.com), Ask (www.ask.com), and Vivisimo (www.vivisimo.com). Yahoo! (www.yahoo.com) is slightly different, being a search directory rather than a search engine, but it is one of the largest guides to the web.

Undertaking a search using any of the search engines or directories appears to be very straightforward: You type in what you're looking for and click on the "Search" or "Go" button. The result: Thousands of sites are returned. To work your way through this mass of information could take hours of valuable time. Possibly the first dozen or so entries may include what you want, and are more than likely to, but they very well may not. So, how can you make your searching more effective?

The judicious use of quotation marks is an essential part of successful Internet searching. If you search for "Brooklyn Pier fire," using quotation marks, search engines will treat the words as an exact phrase and you will get hits.

If you don't use the quotation marks you will get thousands of hits.

You can also use what are called Boolean operators to undertake more complex and focused searches. The most important of these are AND, OR, and NOT: instead of AND you can usually use "+," and for NOT use "–." Therefore, using "Pier" + Brooklyn fire will search for the exact phrase "Pier" with the word "Brooklyn," but not the word "fire," in the same article. Parentheses can also be used together with the Boolean operators. "(Pier OR West) Pier" + Brooklyn, for example, will search for entries that include either "Pier" or "West Pier" and the word "Brooklyn."

An asterisk (*) is used as a wild card when making a search. It stands for one or more letters, or none. Some search engines require a minimum number of letters to the left of the asterisk, two or three. Therefore "Robert*" will find "Robert," "Roberts," "Robertson," and so forth. "Wil*son" will find "Wilson," "Willson," and "Wilkinson."

Searching for information online is easy so long as you develop the mind and methods of a detective. You need to translate your problem into a language that can be used to search the Internet: effectively, a series of keywords and symbols. You could try something like "Richard Spears" + (married OR marriage) + Sutton + Surrey. There are a number of useful keywords for genealogical searches apart from "genealogy" itself: ancestors, descendants, family history, birth/born, marriage/married, death/died.

You, too, can add to the mass of Information available on the Internet by starting your own website. See IDEA 38, Publishing on the web.

Try another idea...

"The Internet is so big, so powerful and pointless that for some people it is a complete substitute for life."
ANDREW BROWN

Defining idea...

"Basic research is what I am doing when I don't know what I am doing."
WERNHER VON BRAUN
(1912–1977)

Defining idea...

225

Last, remember that there is sometimes a difference between US English and UK English, so watch your spelling: center/centre, laborer/labourer, and the like. See *Finding Your Roots Online* by Nancy Hendrickson and *Plugging into Your Past* by Rick Crume for more tips.

How did it go?

Q   **Will my searches find information posted on newsgroups and e-mail groups?**

A   *Sometimes these items need to be accessed directly once you know their URL, as do many online databases. These include such things as online telephone directories, image libraries, street directories, and library catalogs. Google has a facility that allows you to search specific newsgroups, by subject or author.*

Q   **The family name I'm researching is Cook. You can guess what the problem is! What should I do?**

A   *Yes! Make sure every search you make includes "–chef" "–food" (i.e., NOT chef, NOT food). If a celebrity shares the name you are searching for then make sure you remove them, too—so, for example, "Spears NOT Britney" is called for.*

Avoid becoming a drag

Being an avid history chaser doesn't mean you inevitably become the local bore who everybody avoids. Follow these simple rules and you can remain quite normal.

People with what seems to be an obsessive compulsion are often viewed with suspicion by others. So you need to retain the veneer of normality, no matter how exciting your research might be.

Many hobbies are group activities. For example, when going to sports games, you share the emotions, passions, and experiences of watching a game with thousands of other people. And, of course, it's action-packed—things are always changing and you have players and their actions to discuss, plus, of course, the views and opinions of the commentators, and immediate feedback on the game via TV, radio, newspapers, and magazines. In contrast, the researching of your family history is generally a solitary occupation, with you as a single lone detective plowing your way through a variety of records trying to fulfill your current goal or locate that elusive ancestor.

Here's an idea for you... **Find out where and when genealogy or local history meetings or fairs are held near you. One thing you can be sure of is that all the people attendings will be brimming with enthusiasm and eager to swap ideas. As a bonus, you might also find books and periodicals on sale that would never have otherwise come to your attention.**

Researching the lives and times of your forebears, and the aspects of history that surrounded them, allows you to have a much deeper understanding of who you are, but there's the rub—it is who you are. As we are all unique individuals, each with our own ancestry, the minutest details of your family history are interesting and special to you, but only to you; you may be the only one who is fascinated and passionate about it. Very few of us are lucky enough to have all our ancestors leading action-packed lives that are interesting to the general population. Sadly, most of my ancestors led fairly humdrum lives and most of their activities are certainly only of interest to me. This of course does not diminish the passion, importance, and satisfaction that I feel in knowing about my family's past.

Researching your family tree is a great excuse for organizing a family reunion, providing an ideal opportunity to renew or make family acquaintances. It's much better than waiting for a wedding or a funeral, which is often the only time that you might meet your cousins, and it offers you an environment where you can talk about your ancestors to people who will (probably) be interested in your quest. On top of that, you will also be able to catch up on the lives and times of your living relatives, putting the present family into perspective and capturing some oral history at the same time. Even here, though, you should apply a cardinal rule in avoiding geek status—listen very carefully to people and gauge what interest they truly have in the subject.

Family trees and their notes can be difficult to interpret unless you thoroughly follow what you are looking at—which is not always easy to do. So, if you wish to update the different branches of your extended family regularly, then try to present the information in a concise and interesting format. If you have really whetted someone else's appetite, they can always ask you for more information or give you a helping hand with the research.

Get your artistic side into action and scrapbook your research. Using your imagination, you could compile an archive that would engage even the most prosaic family members. For sheer inspiration, see IDEA 40, *Creative scrapbooking*.

Try another idea...

Try to seek out like-minded people to communicate with in the extensive world of family and local history. People who have the same interests as you do will help you extend your knowledge and expertise, plus you can share your experiences with them and enjoy celebrating each other's achievements. Making yourself knowledgeable in your field means that people will seek you out to ask for your help and advice. Get involved with your local society—even if you don't have any interests in the area—because you will be mixing with people who share your passion.

We are all different and enjoy different pastimes and activities. Some of us enjoy watching sports, reading books, climbing mountains, or walking our dogs—and some of us enjoy researching our family and local history.

"You are never too old to set another goal or to dream a new dream."
C. S. LEWIS (1898–1963), academic and writer

Defining idea...

Q   **How can I try to get my husband and children interested in their family history?**

A   *Try to do only very small bits of research while they are with you so that they don't become too bored. For example, if you're out on a summer afternoon ramble, don't spend too long looking for family graves in the local graveyard. Doing some background work on your own before you go can help you quickly locate said graves—which is much more likely to impress and enthuse the rest of the family. However, you may just have to face the fact that although they may be interested in some of your discoveries, golf or computer games may have a higher priority in their lives.*

Q   **How do I deal with relatives who have fixed ideas about their ancestry and do not seem to relate to the information I've gained through extensive research using primary resources?**

A   *Usually when someone has very fixed ideas of "the truth" about their family's ancestry, it is very difficult to persuade them to consider any other alternatives. I have a relative who is convinced that the family is descended from English royalty, even to the extent that they have changed their name to reflect their "inherited status." However, during my extensive research of that family, I have not been able to find any evidence to confirm this line of thought. So, until I do, I quietly treat it as an unconfirmed family story. I suggest you do the same.*